She
The Image of God

Lenne' Hunt

author**HOUSE**®

AuthorHouse™
1663 Liberty Drive
Bloomington, IN 47403
www.authorhouse.com
Phone: 833-262-8899

© 2024 Lenne' Hunt. All rights reserved.

No part of this book may be reproduced, stored in a retrieval system, or transmitted by any means without the written permission of the author.

Published by AuthorHouse 02/12/2024

ISBN: 979-8-8230-2137-1 (sc)
ISBN: 979-8-8230-2136-4 (hc)
ISBN: 979-8-8230-2135-7 (e)

Library of Congress Control Number: 2024901897

Print information available on the last page.

Bible Sources:

Amplified Bible AMP
Common English Bible CEB
English Standard Version ESV
International Children's Bible ICB
The Message MSG
Modern English Version MEV
Names of God NOG
New American Standard Bible NASB
New English Translation NET
New International Version NIV
New Living Translation NLT
New Revised Standard Version, Anglicized NRSVA
The Living Bible TLB
The Passion Translation TPT
Tree of Life Version TLV

Any people depicted in stock imagery provided by Getty Images are models, and such images are being used for illustrative purposes only. Certain stock imagery © Getty Images.

This book is printed on acid-free paper.

Interior Image Credit: Abraham Gonzalez Fernandez, Trendsetter Images, Tatyana Tomsickova, xavierarnau
Cover Image Credit : Jasmina007

Because of the dynamic nature of the Internet, any web addresses or links contained in this book may have changed since publication and may no longer be valid. The views expressed in this work are solely those of the author and do not necessarily reflect the views of the publisher, and the publisher hereby disclaims any responsibility for them.

Contents

Acknowledgments ix
Prologue xi

Chapter 1 Life's Important Questions 1
Chapter 2 What's in a Name? 10
Chapter 3 The Face of Joy and Delight, the Face of Love 15
Chapter 4 The Apple and the Tree 41
Chapter 5 Twisted Eve 63
Chapter 6 To Mother, a Verb 83
Chapter 7 The Great Why 103
Chapter 8 Your Other Big Whys 110
Chapter 9 Ezer 123
Chapter 10 Do-Over: Redemption and Restoration 146

Appendix 161
Glossary 163
Resources for Further Mother Heart/Mother God
Exploration 165

For the women who have graced my life with their own,
I pray that within these pages you
come face-to-face with God
and are met with the gaze of Love which looks at you
with the full affection, adoration, love, and approval of heaven.

Acknowledgments

This book began with a conversation among friends about a conference we were planning for women. I never dreamed at that point that it would become *She*, but the Trinity had plans They hadn't shared with me yet. When I think back to those early conversations, what comes to mind is gratitude for Robin Thompson, Sherry Jennings, and Dana Andrechyn. They offered their good hearts, the ponderings of their souls, their intimacy with God, and their friendship—such valuable and precious treasures.

As tends to happen, those conversations led to others, and more dear friends lent their ears and their voices to the collective symphony. My warm thanks and deep appreciation go to Melissa Kimball, Brooke Phillips, Sandra Sheih, and my mom Edna Hunt.

I also want to acknowledge the women whose own exploration into the femininity of God, the mother heart of God, and its reflection in the lives of women has informed and enriched my own journey. Thank you for your courage and transparency: Sarah Bessey, Susan Harrison (The Mother God Experiment), Anne Lamott, Marg Mowczko, and Carolyn Custis James. And to those at Wild at Heart/Become Good Soil—John and Stasi Eldredge and Morgan and Cherie Snyder—you are such a gift to the earth, trailblazers who point us to a deeply relational God and who speak to the Trinity's power to restore our hearts.

Prologue

> Woman is the crown of creation—the most
> intricate, dazzling creature on earth. She has a
> crucial role to play, a destiny of her own.
> —John and Stasi Eldredge, *Captivating:
> Unveiling the Mystery of a Woman's Soul*

I find myself wondering about your reaction to that quote from *Captivating*. In full honesty, mine is a bit of "Oh come on now, isn't that a bit dramatic and overblown?" mixed with "God, could that be true? Please let that be true." Then, just for good measure, swirl in a dose of "If that's true, then Houston, we have a problem!"

As a life and relationship coach, I spend most of my time walking alongside people in seasons of pain, loss, turmoil, and confusion. Many of the women I journey with are in the midst of soul-crushing, emotionally abusive marriages. In a relationship that is supposed to be the most intimate expression of love, these women are met instead with control and disregard, with name-calling, raging, and cold silent distance. They live with financial and sexual abuse as well as emotional unavailability which leave them feeling lonely and unseen. And they are told in words and behaviors that they have little worth and value. They are embarrassed to have been loved so poorly as though that is a reflection of some lack in them.

It is no wonder then that by the time they come to me, these women are less than they once were. The natural reaction to abuse is to shrink back—you make yourself as small as possible in order to avoid attracting the other's abusiveness. Not only have these women lost parts of themselves, but the parts that remain are twisted out of shape. I often hear from them that they don't like who they have become. Pushed to the brink of their emotional control, they are ashamed of their sometimes out-of-control reactions. Their stories resonate with my own as I remember living in a relationship like that.

The story of your life might contain elements of abuse or toxicity like the ones I've described. But even if it doesn't, there are many other things that can hinder and delay our coming into the fullness of God, the truth of our own identity, and the fullness of life. You might have a tale of woe that stems from your childhood. Or perhaps you've lived as an unmentored woman—with no one to speak into your feminine soul and no guide for your journey of becoming. Or maybe it is simply that you've lived some time in this world of confusion. It is a world where Eve and her daughters have often been targeted by the evil one, sometimes wearing the guise of various authority figures (from civil government to church leadership, school officials, and workplace bosses) and sometimes speaking through the voice of wounded Adam and his sons. The evil one has even succeeded in turning us against our sisters—in judgment and competition, in jealousy and anxiety.

The path to healing the hearts of women has many steps. Among them is the walk back to who we are—picking up pieces of ourselves we have lost along the way or which perhaps we've never seen clearly due to the lies that our hearts have believed in moments of pain. We also work on understanding what has happened to us by exploring the story of our lives. And there is a discovery of new aspects of self which will be needed in the next season of our journey. To live in a way that is authentic, that is truly life, we must be willing to wrestle with life's important questions. And we must go back to the beginning, to the way things were supposed to be once upon a time. I invite you to come with me to explore the journey of your life and of our collective experience as women.

Chapter 1

Life's Important Questions

───────────── ❦ ─────────────

It's hard to shake the feeling of otherness, telling me I am a tourist in my own life. *Growing up in America, Princess Izumi will never be truly Japanese,* an imperial biographer recently wrote. I faced the same in Mount Shasta. *Izumi will never be truly American.* Truth? Sometimes I question if I should even be a princess of Japan. If I am laying claim to something that isn't mine. Maybe I will never be Japanese enough. My throat is scratchy, and I curl my fingers into my palms. No. This is my right. I was raised in America, but my father is the Crown Prince, and Japanese values are still a deep pool within me. Entrenched in my blood. People can say what they want. That I am not enough. They can talk, but I stay silent, quietly digging deeper, pulling up my roots, satiating my thirst. (Emiko Jean, *Tokyo Dreaming*)

It's an odd question, isn't it—*Who are you*? At a party, among people we don't know, someone says, "Tell me about yourself." Or perhaps in a business context, on the first day of a new job, a boss might instruct us to introduce ourselves. Even more daunting, how do you write your bio on an online dating site? How do you even begin to capture the essence of who you are? By the hats you wear, the roles you play, the culture around you, or the product of your hands and of your heart? What is the difference between who you are and what you do?

My hope for you is that your heart would be settled in knowing who you are.

So much of life gets hung up on that unanswered question. Perhaps like many of us, you've had the experience of feeling like you're living someone else's life and not your own. That can happen for lots of reasons. Maybe you were raised in a family culture defined by control or an unhealthy measure of authoritarianism that left little room for independent thought or choice. Alternately you might have been raised by a family with little to no structure, a family that felt chaotic and offered little mentoring or guidance. Sometimes we manage to come through childhood with a fairly clear understanding of who we are, but we lose ourselves in adulthood whether that's due to the sheer busyness of life, the addition of spouses and children, or finding ourselves in an abusive relationship that twists us out of shape. There are many paths to confusion. But no matter how you get there, feeling lost to yourself has painful and damaging consequences.

In the journey of becoming or the journey of recovering ourselves, there is a basic truth that forms the building blocks for our lives. Whether we are plants or animals, wooly mammoths or humans, we are the product of the DNA of our parents. There's no getting away from it. Nothing springs to life from

She

nothing. We come to life out of the union of maternal and paternal DNA and the breath of life that brings us into being. Before we can know who *we* are, we have to know about those who came before us.

Adopted children experience this naturally, often feeling a strong drive to know about their birth parents. That curiosity is born from the intuitive sense that there's more to their story than what they know. How and where does your story begin? You might think the answer is found in the tale of your birth parents, but that isn't actually your true beginning. All of us are more ancient than the decades of our lives on earth. That's a helpful truth to know since one of the things I want to acknowledge up front is that for many people, the concept of mothers and fathers is very painful. For many of us, life with either or both of our parents went badly wrong at some point—perhaps in neglectfulness of our physical being or of our hearts or abusiveness or rejection or a critical spirit. So this thought that the beginning of our story is much more ancient than our mothers and fathers is a thought full of hope.

My hope is that you will come to know where you came from, where your story begins.

Then there is the great *why* of your life. Does your existence have a reason, a purpose, and a meaning, and would it matter whether or not you lived in that purpose? Can life be truly lived without it? What does your life affect beyond just yourself?

My hope is that you will find the joy that comes from knowing why you exist.

We often encounter a version of these questions in late childhood and early adolescence as people begin to ask us what we want to *be* when we grow up. That is usually followed by questions about what we'll major in during college or what sort of job path we see for ourselves. As a college professor, I saw many students struggle with those questions. When people ask what we want to be when we grow up, there's an assumption that our *work*, our doing, will be an expression of our *being.* It's not a terrible assumption but is much to ask of an eighteen-year-old, especially one who has never settled the who-am-I and where-do-I-come-from issues. But perhaps a larger part of the confusion is because the great *why* of our lives may have little to do with what we eventually do for work and more to do with the larger issue of how we live and how we interact with others.

All of that—all of the answers to who you are, why you are, and where you came from—all of that mystery is contained within the heart of God. To know ourselves and the story of our lives, we must know the Trinity. Your DNA traces back to them, and because of that, God must be your North Star. Your life will not make sense without it.

The Quarry from Which You Were Dug (Isaiah 51:1)

Once upon a time (that's the beginning of all good stories!), long before time began, before the land and the sea, and before the galaxies with all their celestial bodies, God existed. And in that existence, we are immediately confronted with a great mystery: This is one God, made up of a Trinity. If that is all we ever know about God, it is enough to fill our hearts with wonder. How can one be three and three be one?

Scripture indicates that each of the three members of the Trinity has Their own mind, will, and heart. This is most clearly seen in the garden of Gethsemane where Jesus is in distress over what He knows is coming next. In great dread, and needing the comfort and companionship of His Father, Jesus makes this telling statement, "If there is any way for this cup, this coming suffering, to pass from Me, let it be so. But if not, I choose what You want, Father, not what I want." Can you hear that? *Not what*

I want. Not my will. This is Jesus, deferring His own desires and feelings to a greater plan, authored by His Father.

This immediately brings us to the first two truths of the Trinity: *God is relational* and *God desires union.* As a triune being, the Trinity exists in intimacy, fellowship, and communion with Themselves. It is Their nature to want relationship. It is Their nature to desire union, which in Hebrew is called *echad* and in English, *one flesh-ness*. The picture here is of three distinct beings *choosing*, out of love and honor, to bring Themselves in sync with one another. There is a mutual deferring and leaning into. In a culture where love is the operating system, each member of the Trinity can give way to the others, trusting that the others will also love and honor Them in return. Love makes it safe to bend into one another. This is the culture of God, the way of the Trinity, which means that it is the pattern for everything that flows from God.

Contained within the three-in-one mystery is another that is not often spoken of in Christian circles. It is this: as much as the Trinity includes Father (Abba) and Son (Jesus), it also includes Mother (Amma). Don't panic; just breathe while I explain. You probably expected me to say Father, Son, and Holy Spirit. So why did I include Mother God instead? The answer is found in Genesis 1. This is our initial introduction to the feminine aspect of the Trinity *in the person of the Holy Spirit*. Hebrew is a language that uses gender-specific pronouns—a fact that doesn't necessarily matter so much when applied to objects but that has purposeful intent when applied to people (or in this case, God). *HaKodesh,* a noun written in feminine form, is the Hebrew term for the Holy Spirit. But this isn't just a grammatical issue. We also see the femininity of God in the behavioral description of the Spirit in Genesis 1:2 (NASB),

> And the earth was a formless and desolate emptiness, and darkness was over the surface

of the deep, *and the Spirit of God was hovering over the surface of the waters.* (emphasis mine)

This word *hovering* is the same word used in Deuteronomy 32:11, describing God as one who protects and cares for Israel "like an eagle stirs up her nest, that flutters over her young" (MEV). We are seeing here an image of God as a mother hen brooding over her chicks. This is a reference repeated many times in scripture. The once-upon-a-time of Genesis paints a picture of life about to be born and Mother God in labor to deliver it into the world and to keep it safe. Our next feminine view of God comes just a few verses later,

> Then God said, "Let Us make man in Our image, after Our likeness! Let them rule over the fish of the sea, over the flying creatures of the sky, over the livestock, over the whole earth, and over every crawling creature that crawls on the land." God created humankind in His image, *in the image of God He created* him, male and *female* He created them. (Genesis 1:26–27 TLV, emphasis mine)

As it turns out, God is both *He* and *She* and also more than either—something John Eldredge describes as *gender-full.* I realize that in some circles this might be considered heresy, sacrilege, or feminism gone wrong. But scripture says it very clearly. For women to exist in the world, the Godhead must contain the feminine. *You cannot be made in the image of something that does not exist.* The only other option is to contradict scripture and conclude that women were not made in the image of God or were somehow made less in that image than men—an option that leads to a host of terrible beliefs and behaviors.

I realize that this may be jarring, but if you allow yourself to

She

wander here even for a bit, you'll find that things make more sense than they might without this view of the Trinity. I also realize that most of you don't know me personally, so I want to offer a small window into my heart in the hopes it might set yours more at ease. My love and respect for God are immense, and the revelation of the Trinity's fatherhood has changed my life (I even wrote a book about it!). Nothing said here is meant to diminish God as Father or to detract from the Trinity as the template for masculinity.

At the same time, you surely know that God is more than gender while containing the pattern and being the pattern for what we experience on the earth as gender. Both maleness and femaleness are equally part of the image of God. This is what scripture says. When we embrace that view, we begin to see why the Trinity chose gender as a means to display Their identity. Life isn't created without both a father and a mother, each having equally important and essential roles.

This is also why the earthly expression of the culture of heaven takes the form of a family and a house. These are symbols that teach us about the relationship of the created and the creator—that humanity is more than just an art project. We are designed to be the daughters and sons of God with all the intimate familiarity that implies. The symbols of house and family illustrate the essence of love and point us to an ultimate destiny at the end of the age.

We also find in these symbols a view of the Trinity itself. It is hard to put this in words so I'll ask that you try to imagine this scene. Before we existed, the Trinity sat and talked among themselves. Father, Mother/Holy Spirit, and Son. They all gathered around some heavenly table and discussed things. They loved one another and enjoyed each other's company. Each sang the other's praises, supported the other's desires, and participated in creative acts together. This divine family existed together in companionable silence and warm fellowship. They had a common desire which was to enlarge Their circle of community in order to share Their love and companionship. This was the desire that caused humankind to exist.

Making humanity in the image of the Trinity involved representing different aspects and qualities of God, but also the way in which the members of the Trinity fit together in a relationship. Women are a physical expression of a central aspect of the Trinity—made to be life bearers, tender nurturers, intimate lovers, and fierce protectors. Without women, creation itself was incomplete and Adam was not yet *good*.

For some people, this may seem like much ado about nothing. A common response is to say that we should agree that gender-based pronoun language isn't important; for example, portraying God solely as *He* or referring to humankind as *mankind* should be sufficient. History tells us otherwise. Our own experience tells us otherwise. It is much too easy to go from an all-encompassing *he* to a version of that which only includes men. If we've learned anything from the social unrest our country has faced in recent years, it is the importance of the see-one, be-one principle. People struggle to feel valued, included, safe, and represented when there is no view of someone like themselves within the authority structure that is over them. A similar effect occurs when language, optics, and portrayals of success leave out a group of people or section of society. To represent the Trinity devoid of a feminine presence is to suggest that women are not truly made in the image of God, and as such, are lesser in some way than men. This in turn leads to a cascade of effects. For example, placing women in a lesser category gives room to limit the rights that are granted to us such as self-advocacy and participation and voice in sculpting the practices of society. This also provides a justification for lower basic standards for the humane treatment of women. All of these things create a substantial assault on self-worth which in turn can lead to the acceptance of abusive treatment. A lesser view of women also robs us of a mentoring role model within the Trinity, making it much more difficult to know who we are.

We will continue to explore this, but for now, I want to sow a seed that will mature as we journey together. Adam and Eve are jointly *humankind* (a better rendering than *mankind*). They are equally human. They are equally created in the image of a Trinity who is big enough to hold the elements of both the masculine and the feminine while being more than either of these concepts. Adam and Eve are endowed with equal amounts of reflected glory—though the aspects of the Trinity they reflect may be different in some ways. Because *equal* does not necessarily mean identical but rather having the same value, we can say that men and women have equal gifting, equally important destiny and calling, and equal favor and affection in the heart of God. They are also equally responsible for the fall of Eden where they failed one another as well as the God who gave them life.

These things shouldn't have to be said. They are obvious in scripture, in the story God is telling. And yet one of the consequences of the fall is that the great deceiver was given room to obscure truth and sow divisiveness. This creates the condition that has been our experience ever since: a house divided against itself cannot stand. It is time for the truth to be told and the house to be healed.

Chapter 2

What's in a Name?

---------- ❦ ----------

Carve your name on hearts, not tombstones.
—Shannon L. Alder

When you love someone, you say their name different.
Like it's safe inside your mouth.
—Jodi Picoult

As we journey to understand who we are in our femininity, it's helpful to look at what we know of the *She-ness* of God. Though this revelation begins in the person of the Holy Spirit, it doesn't stop there. In scripture, names usually tell us something about the character of people and places. For example, Jerusalem means "the city of peace," Bethel is "the house of God," David means *beloved*, and Noah is *rest*. So one of the ways that the Trinity teaches us about Their nature is through names; for example, *Yeshua* reveals Jesus as *Yahweh Saves*, *Yahweh Rapha* tells us of *God who heals,* and *Yahweh Jireh* promises that *God will see and provide.*

Among the names of God is El Shaddai, traditionally translated as *God Almighty*, yet the root of this name, *shad*, means breasts. This emphasis gives us *God, the breasted*

She

one—another evidence and manifestation of God in the feminine. Biblical scholar Cyrus Scofield calls the traditional translation of El Shaddai as *God Almighty* a "regrettable" thing. Believing that *the Breasted One* is a far better rendering, he explains that "as a fretful, unsatisfied babe is not only strengthened and nourished from the mother's breast but also is quieted, rested, satisfied, so El Shaddai is that name of God which sets him forth as the Strength-giver and Satisfier of his people." [1]

This view of God is obscured when we don't have the literal representation of the Breasted One who is Mother to us, and in that mothering, gives nourishment and creates peace, rest, security, a place of warmth, and a sense of belonging. This is the aspect of God that is life-bearing, life-producing, and creative. It is echoed in God's design of women which has led Morgan Snyder to call El Shaddai, "the Source of the pleasure, security, rest, peace, and nourishment that robust femininity was meant to provide."

A feminine image of God is often startling to the modern-day church, but it really shouldn't come as any surprise. Of course, some of the names of God should contain feminine imagery if God contains as much feminine as masculine—a Trinity who creates women as well as men in Their image. Why make Eve at all unless her existence was necessary to help more fully represent the nature of God?

When the Trinity reveals Themselves this way, what are They telling us about who They are, and who They are *to us*? Earlier I wrote that the Trinity had the desire to share their love and companionship and to enlarge Their circle of community. What we are seeing here is the nature of love. Love is creative and procreative, wanting to reproduce itself in another. You see, it isn't just that God is relational in some general sense. God has a particular heart that comes from being Father and

---

[1] . Cyrus Ingerson Scofield, *The Scofield Bible Commentary* (Oxford University Press, 1917).

Mother. This was true before we ever existed. It is also the truth that *caused us to exist.* Our relational God who exists as a Father and Mother, wanted to expand Their family. The Trinity wanted more children for Themselves, and a bride for Their Son.

From the beginning of the story God is writing, the Trinity uses the imagery of family to represent Their own being—a family that requires a mother to conceive and give birth to children. Here we come, once again, back to the mother heart of God. Mother God, *El Shaddai,* God with breasts, is the one who holds us close against Her skin so that we rest in Her warmth and are comforted by Her heartbeat. El Shaddai is the one whose very essence feeds us—keeping us alive by Her very being. Our lives were formed in Her; we were carried and developed in Her. Or as Paul writes, "In God we live, move, and exist" (Acts 17:28 CEB). These are the breasts against which we lay so that we can gaze into the eyes of love. This is what God offers—comfort, care, nourishment, warmth, adoration. This is who God is, El Shaddai, and who God is to us and for us.

> *El Shaddai, help me to know You this way. Bring me into Your care. Holy Spirit, let Your comforting ease my fears. Let me be fed by Your very essence—drinking in the milk of Your life force. Let me see the love in Your eyes as You hold me close to Your warmth. Help me to know rest in Your embrace.*

Perhaps it is a new thought for you that the Trinity is as feminine as They are masculine. After all, pretty much everything we're taught about God uses the pronoun *he.* We know God as Father, and He is. We know God as Jesus, the Son, and He is. But there is more to God. As we've seen, this is reflected most clearly in the names of God which are written in the feminine form: El Shaddai and the Holy Spirit (Ruach HaKodesh). But the other way the Trinity reveals their feminine nature is through scriptural imagery. For example, pay attention to the language in verses like these (emphasis is mine):

> From whose *womb* comes the ice?
>
> Who *gives birth* to the frost of heaven? (Job 38:29 TLV)
>
> But those who did welcome him, those who believed in his name, he authorized to become God's children, born not from blood nor from human desire or passion, *but born from God.* (John 1:12 CEB)
>
> The God *who gave you birth.* (Deuteronomy 32:18 AMP)
>
> Let me dwell in Your tent forever; Let me take refuge *in the shelter of Your wings.* (Psalm 61:4 AMP)
>
> "Jerusalem, Jerusalem ... How often I've ached to embrace your children, *the way a hen gathers her chicks under her wings*, and you wouldn't let me." (Matthew 23:37 MSG)
>
> When Israel was a child I loved him, and out of Egypt I called my son. The more I called them, the more they went from me ... Yet it was I who taught Ephraim to walk, I took them up in my arms; but they did not know that I healed them. I led them with cords of human kindness, with bands of love. *I was to them like those who lift*

> *infants to their cheeks. I bent down to them and fed them ... My compassion grows warm and tender.* (Hosea 11:1–4, 8 NRSVA)

When we cut ourselves off from this revelation of God, we miss so much of what God offers us. The Trinity wanted us to know all of Them, even as They know all of us. This is true intimacy. There are qualities in the feminine that are not as clearly seen and experienced in the masculine. For example, Father God, Abba, possesses tenderness and nurturing qualities. Reflected in the design of men, healthy masculinity certainly contains those things as well but offers them differently than femininity does. It isn't that the masculine and feminine of God are at odds or are opposites; they simply offer different expressions of the heart of the Trinity.

God always intended that we would be Their children. They designed us with that in mind. The Trinity is our Father and our Mother, and we are Their daughters. Not merely God's creation, but Their kin. Humanity's design includes the relational identity of being sons and daughters. Something in us cries out for our parents and something in God calls out to Their children. This is the ultimate answer to the question of where we come from. We come from the heart of Love, from the intimacy of the Trinity, from Their desire to share Their love. Who we are as women is birthed from this DNA. We are created by Love, in love, and for love. We are designed to be tangible embodiments and reflections of the feminine aspects of God.

And that brings us to the creation of humankind.

Chapter 3

The Face of Joy and Delight, the Face of Love

It is only with the heart that one can see rightly.
What is essential is invisible to the eyes.
—Antoine de Saint-Exupery

On the sixth day of creation, the Trinity changes up Their creative process. Up 'til now, each element of creation came into being through God's spoken word. But midway through the sixth day, God stops merely speaking and takes a hands-on approach. What we see here is a stunning moment of intimacy.

Scripture says that God formed Adam from the dust of the earth. Let's consider that. The God of all that is and ever will be. The God of infinite power and might and honor and glory—*that* God chooses to get His hands dirty, to kneel in the dust as a potter leans over the clay, and to form that dust into the body of a man. Understand that God didn't have to do it this way. The Trinity could have just spoken us into being like They did with everything else. It would have been enough. But something else is going on here.

Lenne' Hunt

    This is love and desire at work, not a dispassionate scientist nor a God far away out there, but Imanu'El, God *with* us. There is something *up close and personal* about this moment in the story. God kneels in the dust, shaping it, forming it, and tending to it in order to bring life out of it (a charge the Trinity will later pass on to Adam and Eve).

    At some point, Adam's body is perfectly formed, perfect yet without life. So in another act of intimacy, God breathes life into Adam. Again take a moment to picture this in your mind's eye. God kneels in the dirt over Adam's body, leaning in until they are face to face and the literal breath of God can enter Adam's nose and mouth (the very first instance of CPR!). The implication is immediate—God breathes and Adam comes to life. His eyes open for the first time and what does Adam see? It is the face of Love, leaning over him.

Photo by Abraham Gonzalez Fernandez via iStock

Those of you who are parents know what it is like to see your child for the first time. Whether this is a child born of your body or one that comes to you through adoption, this first glimpse of them is a thing of wonder. You've waited all this time for your child to arrive. You've thought about them, planned for them, and made room in your house and in your heart for their existence. And there they are! Without thinking, your face begins to smile in joy and delight, in love and wonder. You count the fingers and toes, wanting to memorize every detail. The cost of waiting and longing, even the pain of birth itself is eclipsed by joy. So now imagine the experience of the child, new to the world, opening his or her eyes to the sight of your face, the face of love.

This was Adam's first experience of life. In the moment of his first breath, Adam saw on the face of God that he was loved, adored, delighted in, and wanted. He knew because he was staring into the face of Love, that Father God was a safe place—a source of warmth and affection. And because of that, all was well with him and in the world. This is Eve's story as well—also made by Father's own hands, not out of mud as Adam was, but from a rib taken from Adam's own body. She too must come to life through Trinity's breath, awakening to Love's face.

This is the power of love's gaze, the power of what we now call attachment, of being seen by the eyes of love and through the eyes of love. It's as though the parent's face serves as a mirror for the child, reflecting back to them who they are—beloved, wanted, chosen, adored. This was Father's gift to Adam and Eve.

Photo by Trendsetter Images via iStock

Abba, Amma, let me sit in that moment with You again. Help me feel the joy in Your heart over my existence. Let me remember, as though for the first time, the warmth of being held by You as You love me, as You make room for me in Your heart and in the world. Holy Spirit, help me to feel again that there is a place where I belong—a place where I am seen, adored, and wanted, where I am the object of Your heart's affection. Help my heart to find its home in You.

The need to attach to another, to find acceptance, belonging, safety, welcome, love, and regard is a biological imperative written into our DNA. God made it literally part of our design. It is one of our survival mechanisms as wee babes. As silly as it may sound, babies of all species are cute for a reason—it draws adult attention and care. The cuteness of a child along with those heart-piercing cries are meant to create attachment *because babies will die without it.* Hear the imperative in that. Our very lives depend on others offering care, nurture, and attention. This is why this drive is so very strong and reaches the core of us. Beyond infancy, even when we are well able to feed and clothe ourselves and up until the day we die, we still live with this strong desire for attachment. Love's gaze is what we were made for, and without it, our hearts wither and die. It isn't just that attachment is essential for the survival of our bodies. The well-being of our souls also depends on it.

We know that attachment affects three major aspects of our souls: our beliefs about our own value and worth, our beliefs about the nature of others, and our understanding of the world at large. It works like this. For attachment to go well, parents must *consistently* and *appropriately* (something called *attunement*) meet a child's needs. If that happens, the message the child learns is that they are worth seeing and worth being taken care of. It creates an expectation that others can be trusted to see us and meet us—we are safe with them and will receive care from them. Then by extension, the child also comes to expect that the world is a safe and good place which they can explore, knowing that the parents are a safe base they can return to at any moment of anxiety or distress. This is called *secure* attachment.

However, if the *consistently* and *appropriately* conditions are not met, insecure attachment develops. This can take any of three forms. *Avoidant* attachment occurs when parents consistently do not meet children's needs. The message is clear: you are not worth attending to; your feelings do not have value; and you cannot count on us to help you feel seen, comforted, and safe. This can create a shut-down and inappropriately independent emotional style. The child has learned not to take their needs to others because there is no expectation that others will come through for them.

In *anxious-ambivalent* attachment, the key dynamic is inconsistency from the parents. They sometimes meet the child in their need and they sometimes do it appropriately, but the child has difficulty predicting which version of their parents they will encounter. If I cry, will my parents come? And if they come to meet me, will they correctly discern that I am hungry and feed me or will they mistakenly think I need my diaper changed and ignore my hunger? Understand here that we're not talking about a one-time interaction between parents and children, but rather a pattern of responding and reacting. Children may experience this as very conditional love and develop an anxious pursuit as they look for the magic key to securing their parents' affection. This often causes them to live with a fear of abandonment.

The last type, *disorganized* attachment, shares characteristics of both avoidant and anxious but with the added elements of confusion and fear. These are children whose relational environment was unpredictable in the sense that parents occasionally showed up as sources of comfort and care but alternated that with times of abuse. The child develops a fearful, perhaps even trauma-based approach to their parents, while still yearning for those occasional moments of tenderness.

Ultimately attachment was meant to be the process by which we come to know who we are. Because we are made in the image of a relational God, true clarity about our identity only comes through *healthy* relationships with the Trinity and with people (most importantly, our parents, spouses, and closest trusted friends). I've emphasized the need for healthy relationships because true love must be what shapes our mirroring of one another. This is because love is the only thing that sees clearly—sees us in a totality that encompasses not just what we've done or our current state of being but rather our innate value. If love isn't what shapes our mirroring, the messages we reflect back to others about their value and identity become corrupted to some degree.

Many people grow up with parents who are deep in their own woundedness and operate from a place of emotional immaturity and underdevelopment. Unfortunately, the nature of being a child is that we often don't grasp that that's what's

She

going on and instead assume that the parental reaction is due to some lack in us. That wounded child gets tucked away in us and forms the core beliefs we hold about ourselves even into our own adulthood. If this sounds familiar to you and if this is something your heart still struggles with, I want to take the time here to say it clearly. When a parent with a healthy and loving heart looks at their child, their heart does *not* say, "I love you, but I'll love you more when you learn how to load the dishwasher and properly conjugate verbs." When their child has disobeyed and eaten not just two cookies but the whole package and now they're throwing up all over the carpet in the living room, a healthy and loving parental heart does *not* say, "I love you, but I'll love you more when you start listening to me, and by the way, don't bother coming to dinner until you clean yourself up." The message of a healthy and loving heart is far simpler. It is just "I love you." Achievement and obedience don't increase love, nor does the lack of them detract from it.

As a simple example of that, let me tell you about my dog Stevie. When he was only two weeks old, the people who owned his mother decided that they had no use for her puppies and they literally threw them in the trash. I wish I could show you the pure fury I feel as I think about that. How dare they? It breaks my heart to write those words and a fierceness rises up from the depths of my being that wants to see them jailed or worse. They called those sweet little puppies *trash* and treated them accordingly. Some kind soul found and rescued the babies out of the trash bin, and they were placed with foster families until they were old enough to be adopted. This is how I enter Stevie's story. I adopted him when he was seven weeks old. Stevie came home with me, slept in my bed, and ate all manner of tasty things including the eggs I cooked for him in the morning. He had toys and blankets, and I eventually even got him a puppy of his own so he'd have a playmate.

Here's the point. Stevie was the same dog when thrown in the trash bin as he was when living his best life in my home. *He* did not change. What changed were the eyes that saw him. One set of eyes viewed Stevie through the lens of inconvenience and annoyance. I viewed him through the lens of love, and it caused me to *set my affection* on him. Love is what he was worth. At that moment, the truth about little Stevie came to light. He is heaven's creation as I am. He, like me, is a reflection of the God who made him—the God who made him out of love and for love. *Stevie's existence was meant to point the world back to God.* The same Trinity who is faithful and loving toward me is faithful and loving toward Stevie and all the rest that They have made. That is what scripture tells us in Psalm 145:13. I'll repeat what I said earlier. If love isn't what shapes our mirroring, the messages we reflect back to others about their value and identity become tainted by woundedness and sin and therefore offer false conclusions.

It is easy to see how our understanding of identity is forged in the fires of attachment. I'm talking here about the deepest of core beliefs concerning our essential worth and character. Have you ever wondered why scripture tells that following each day of creation, God looked over what had been made and pronounced that it was good? What is that moment about? Is the Trinity surprised by Their own creativity? Certainly, we know that can't be the case; They are surprised by nothing. What then is happening in these moments?

I believe that each of these pronouncements serves as benediction and blessing. This is the Trinity releasing identity and approval into every created thing. *Mountains, you are good; waters you are good; antelopes, eagles, minnows, and trees—you are good.* It is a statement of truth, of value, and of essence. It is also a statement of blessing: *You are good and I release you into the world to impact it with your goodness, with your reflection of Our goodness.*

And then we get to the sixth day. The land animals are formed—there is a sense of creation swelling up, of the soundtrack reaching for a crescendo. Then a holy hush falls as though the mountains dare not breathe. All the elements of creation witness God kneeling in the dust to make Adam, and the breath of God, the Spirit of God (Ruach HaKodesh) fills him. You can almost hear the world gasping as this son of God is created right before their very eyes. Even so, there has not yet been the pronouncement of *good*. What is left to come? Then in this final push of creation's birth, God brings Eve out of Adam and fills her with that same Spirit. All of creation breaks into a roar of celebration as the Trinity finally declares that this is good. "You, man and woman, are good, and I release you into the world to impact it with your goodness, with your reflection of Our goodness." Everything that Adam and Eve would come to know about themselves—everything that we today would call *identity*—was rooted in God's pronouncement of blessing over their lives and then revealed and developed in relationship with God and with one another.

The design of heaven is very contrary to the American perspective on identity. Culturally, we've embraced the thought that identity is, and must be, forged independently of others. In the culture of heaven, there is no *independence from others*. God exists as a Trinity, never just one of the three. They are who they are *in relationship*, and Their choice to submit to one another in love does not take away from Them as individuals. Similarly, your identity is bestowed on you by the Trinity and is a reflection of your relatedness to Them. Did you catch that last statement? Your identity and its associated value are a reflection of your relatedness to God. They were forged at your creation in the mind and heart of God long before you arrived here. Your identity and value were created the moment the Trinity *set Their affection on you*. Nothing that you've done since, for better or worse, and nothing that's been done toward you, for better or worse, has the power to alter any of that. Eldredge calls this the *benediction of being* that flows from the mother heart of God.

There is a view of this in scripture from the life of the disciple

John. He is often referred to as "the disciple whom Jesus loved" as though that was how other people saw him. In actuality, no one described John that way in scripture except John himself. So what are we to understand from that? The most important thing to consider in deciphering this is whether John intended to speak comparatively or not, "I am the one whom Jesus loved *more than* others." This is what we're often taught but that isn't what John actually says, nor do I think it is what he's trying to imply.

There is a telling clue that comes to light when we look at the writing of John. When you count the references to love contained in the New Testament, nearly half are found in the Gospel and letters of John. John writes more about love than all of Paul's letters combined and just the Gospel of John alone mentions love more times than the other three gospels taken together. Love becomes the theme of John's life. It is his most compelling experience in his relationship with Jesus.

> Given this context then, we need to revisit John's description of himself as the one whom Jesus loved. I don't think he intended that description to imply any sort of comparison. He was not saying that he had more favor or was loved *more* than the others. John was simply stating what had come to be the overriding truth of his life. He was a man loved by Jesus. That one thing came to form the totality of John's identity. It defined him. Who are you John? I'm one whom Jesus loves. What do you know John? I know love. I know what it is to be arrested by the gaze of Love incarnate. To be bathed in love's embrace, to receive its acceptance, its forgiveness, its grace. Where do you live John? I live in the love of my

She

Father, in the love of His son Jesus. I live in union with the heart of God.[2]

Being the beloved is what came to define John. And it follows from that that if I am beloved, then I am worth loving. Dear daughter, can you hear this?

You
Are
Good.

And you are much loved.

This is your identity, the truth of you

From your very beginning,

Before you'd done a thing,

In your essential essence,

With nothing to prove
and with a glory and magnificence to
your life that cannot be lost.

It is not a matter of opinion; people's words cannot change it.

It is a Truth, spoken by a God who does not lie
and whose authority is unmatched.

Selah (pause and reflect on that).

I am actually recommending that you pause. Let those words sink into your mind, your soul. Give your heart permission to

---

[2]. Lenne' Hunt, *Prisoners of Hope: Finding Refuge, Restoration, and Destiny in the Heart of God* (Destiny Image Europe, 2011).

hear them, to receive them as true and not as *too good to be true*. For most of us, this will produce a course correction in our understanding of ourselves. And if you receive them, these words will change so many things about how you feel about yourself and how you walk through the world and in relationships.

This is a necessary step in our healing because negative expectations learned in childhood of self, others, and the world endure throughout our lives unless we encounter corrective experiences. If our wounds are left unhealed, we become people who think poorly of ourselves, which in turn sets us up to tolerate future unkind behavior from others. We become unhealthy in relationships, either anxiously clinging too hard, avoiding intimacy altogether, or acting like a pushmi-pullyu (anyone remember *Dr. Dolittle*?) as we alternately pursue and then reject others.

If we look at God as a mother and father, scripture is clear that the Trinity desires and offers us a relationship in which secure attachment can develop. The Trinity intimately knows us (Psalm 139)—our every thought, our rising, and our sleeping. They know our needs before we do (Matthew 6:8, 25–34) and pledge that goodness and mercy will pursue us all the days of our lives (Psalm 23:6). This is a God who is available and attuned to us. It is evident in the names of God, Yahweh Jireh—the God who sees us and from the seeing moves to provide for us. Zephaniah 3:17 describes the *Lord* who quiets us with Her love and rejoices over us with singing. This is the one who comes in the midst of our storms, and holding us close to His chest, whispers, "Be still and know that I am God." The *God of tender mercies* described in Luke 1:78–79 is the God who gave "light to those who sit in darkness and in the shadow of death, to guide our feet into the way of peace." And so it goes. The names of God are as endless as the Trinity Themselves.

For my heart, one of the most comforting and powerful descriptions of God is in Isaiah 49 where God explains divine motherhood. Speaking out of the mother heart, El Shaddai, the Breasted One, compares Herself to earthly mothers and says, "Can a mother forget the baby at her breast and have no compassion on the child she has borne? Though she may forget, I will not forget you! See, I have engraved you on the palms of my hands; your walls are ever before me" (Isaiah 49:15–17 NIV). Although *walls* could be interpreted literally as the walls around the city of Jerusalem, figuratively these are the walls of our lives. It is hard to convey the strength of this moment. El Shaddai is saying here that as your Mother, Her very being has been marked and altered by loving you. As is true of all good mothers, you, daughter, are always in Her thoughts, in Her heart. She cannot look at Herself without being reminded of you. That's how fierce and true Her love is for you.

Love always has an additive quality—never detracting from us but instead it enlarges us. The Trinity allowed themselves to be affected by love. We see this in Isaiah 49—this expansiveness of heart that comes from El Shaddai creating and bearing Her daughters. She is your beginning, and Her love and attention have accompanied your every breath.

We might ask how, in God's original plan, were we supposed to encounter the Trinity's love for us. Adam and Eve were brought alive to the literal face of God (can you imagine that!). They physically and emotionally encountered God from their very beginning breath. But what about the rest of us? After Father created the initial creatures (including Adam and Eve), every other generation of beings would come to life in the context of the womb rather than being spoken into being or fashioned from mud. That means that every life arrives on the earth in an immediate relationship with their mom. It's a relationship that is formed at conception and fostered and deepened throughout the pregnancy. The baby hears the mom's heartbeat, is oxygenated through her blood, fed through her blood, and protected in her warmth.

Understand that I'm describing the culture of heaven here;

the experience of the womb is like the experience of being held in God—life and nourishment coming through the blood, heartbeat to heartbeat, protected in the warmth of the Trinity's embrace and provision. Remember again Acts 17:28 (CEB), "In God we live, move, and exist." There is an echo of this in the chorus of "The More I Seek You."

> I want to sit at your feet,
> Drink from the cup in your hand;
> *Lay back against you and breathe, feel your heartbeat.*
> This love is so deep, it's more than I can stand.
> I melt in your peace, it's overwhelming. (Emphasis mine)

There is something about that image of leaning back against another, being enclosed in their heartbeat and in their arms. It is where we look for comfort and also where we want to share joy. It is a place of intimacy and protection and wholeness.

Diane Ackerman writes, "But for a baby in the womb, the mother's heartbeat performs the ultimate cradlesong of peace and plenty; the surf-like waves of her respiration lull and soothe. The womb is a snug, familiar landscape, an envelope of rhythmic warmth, and the mother's heartbeat a steady clarion of safety." In response to Ackerman, Dan Allender connects our experience in the womb with what might be available in our relationship with Mother God:

> I don't recall being in the womb, but I have never considered the peace of that home as deeply and richly until I read [Ackerman's] sea-rhythm, heart-cadence, warm-lullaby words. I am mesmerized by the question: "Is that what I felt?" I cannot know, but I can say that I want what Ackerman pens to be an experience of being so near to God that I can hear the cradlesong of God's heart, the lapping resonance of her breathing, and the

holding ground of her skin surrounding me in divine safety and warmth.[3]

Morgan Snyder carries the culture of heaven past the womb experience and into being fed by Mom. "Being at the breast was meant to be a *saving* experience, filling us like a river overflowing its banks and providing such restful, nourishing pleasure that we receive bodily this revelation ... of a God-centered reality: all is deeply and securely well."[4]

Photo by Tatyana Tomsickova via|Dreamstime.com

The revelation of all being well has long been missing on the earth. Our individual and collective anxiety increases with each step further away from Eden, further away from knowing God as El Shaddai, the one who supplies all that we need for life. When Eve and Adam decided to provide for their own lives and their own hearts' desires, they orphaned themselves from

---

[3] . Sabbath: The Ancient Practices, Thomas Nelson (2010) by Dan B. Allender.
[4] . Laying Roof Shingles in a G-String, Become Good Soil, by Morgan Snyder, https://becomegoodsoil.com/2015/11/11/laying-roof-shingles-in-a-g-string/.

Father and Mother God. They and all their descendants forfeited the sense of being securely held and of having access to such abundant nourishment that we never have to fear lack. We women, especially, tend to live anxiously, striving to control life as a means of protecting ourselves from want, calamity, further abandonment, and unrequited need. The irony runs deep in that. We, who are made in the image of Mother to offer others a sense of well-being, rest, and security, desperately need to be mothered by Her, to be cradled in Her tenderness and fed from Her abundance. We cannot offer others what we have not yet received ourselves. We are hindered in offering the kind of beauty that invites others to rest if our own hearts are mired in anxiety. We are unable to create the sense of security that speaks to others that all is well if we don't yet know that El Shaddai is our *more than enough*. This is what John Eldredge calls the "assurance of abundance."

This issue of the mother heart of God is so much bigger than we have known. We see it in the relationship between two Hebrew words: *racham* and *rechem*. *Racham* means to love deeply, have mercy, be compassionate, and have tender affection and compassion while *rechem* (taken from the word racham) means womb. In *Journey of a Metaphor,* Dr. Phyllis Trible writes,

> God speaks in the first person as a mother about Ephraim, her son: "Is not my child, Ephraim, dear to me? Is not Ephraim the child in whom I delight? ... I think of Ephraim with tenderness. My *heart* yearns for him ... surely I will have *mercy* on Ephraim, says Yahweh." (Jeremiah 31:20)

Then Dr. Trible makes the connection that in this passage from Jeremiah, the word *heart* means *inner parts,* which in several other places in scripture, parallels the word *womb.* The very nature of the womb is defined by love and affection, compassion, and mercy. A pregnant woman who has embraced the role of a mother changes how she lives in order to extend kindness toward the child she carries. She alters her eating and minimizes stress in order to help her body tend to her child, considering the child above herself, anticipating the child's needs, and moving to meet them. The mother speaks to the child in her womb, establishing a relationship and familiarity. She delights in their existence and takes joy in feeling the child's movements within her.

In making Eve and all her kind in the image of Mother God (El Shaddai and the Holy Spirit), the Trinity gives women the privilege of hosting both the atmosphere and the gaze of love. What an honor that is. Whether in the wombs of our physical bodies or in the wombs of our hearts, we can offer the same tender mercy, compassion, affection, and safety as heaven offers us.

I realize that some of you might be having trouble connecting with what I've been describing because perhaps your mother wasn't full of compassion and mercy. She wasn't tender and may not have had affection for you. Your mother may not have rejoiced at her pregnancy with you. Even your time in the womb may have been a hostile environment if your mom struggled with wanting you, or if the circumstances of your birth or conception were difficult for her.

You may never have experienced the gaze of love from your mother or at best, experienced it in an inconsistent and confusing way. In fact, your mother might not have been a mother to you at all except in name only. Or perhaps your mother was some of the things I've described but not all of them. Maybe she has a wounded soul that kept her from fully embracing herself in the role of mother.

If you resonate with that—if you have mother wounds—here is the *really good news*. Your biological mother is not your beginning. She doesn't define the truth of you. She was supposed to support and reflect the truth of you, but in whatever ways that might have gone wrong, it doesn't change the truth: Amma, El Shaddai, Mother God, is over the moon in love with you. She and Abba Father were thrilled to conceive you, to bring your body and your being to completion. Amma God looked forward to the life you would live and delighted to bring you to the earth, a gift from her and Father to us.

> My frame was not hidden from you when
> I was made in the secret place,
> when I was woven together in the depths of the earth.
> Your eyes saw my unformed body;
> all the days ordained for me were written in your book
> before one of them came to be.
> For you created my inmost being; you knit
> me together in my mother's womb.
> (Psalm 139:13, 15–16 NIV)

Imagine the face of Mother God as she looks at you, holds you close, and delights in you. The hard, bad, scary, and painful things that happened in your life do not and cannot change Her delight in you. Pause for a moment and take that in. Imagine that you are the little one in this picture, being held by God, delighted in, cherished, adored, and wanted.

Photo by xavierarnau via iStock

Abba, Amma—You know the wounds I have felt from my earthly parents. And You know the lies that have sprung up in my soul from those wounds—that I am not enough, that I am too much. I should have been a boy. I wasn't wanted or was inconvenient, that there was something shameful in me, that my worth was in doing rather than in being. You know the anxiety of my little girl soul that still cries out in my grown woman's heart. Meet me here Amma, El Shaddai, Ruach HaKodesh, Mama of my beginning. Hold me close and let me feel the contours of Your face and the beat of Your heart. Let my little girl's heart soak up Love's gaze and let it heal me.

The Literalness of El Shaddai

As women, to know ourselves and to understand our place in the world, we have to dive deep into the Trinity's existence as She. What is God saying about the Trinity in using the name El Shaddai, "the strong, many-breasted one"? What does this tell us about who God is and who we are created to be as a reflection of that image? The answer begins with the literalness of the name. What do breasts do? In women, they are functional and not just fashion accessories.

- Breasts keep children alive. Such a basic but core truth in that. There is life in the milk that breasts provide. If you think about the time before technology, or even now in third world countries where powdered milk replacement can be scarce, either a mother's body is able to provide nourishment or the child will die.
- The nourishment breasts provide enables children to grow—more than just live or survive. The Trinity designed a mother's body to produce milk at the rate

the child drinks so that milk production keeps pace with the baby's development. The milk allows development and progression.
- The mother's immune system is shared in the milk she gives her child and so provides physical protection against disease.

Aside from their physical function, there is also the element of warmth, safety, and emotional protection that comes from children being held close to the breast. To be held is the beginning of feeling safe, seen, wanted, and welcome. As babies, we are invited there. Understand the importance of invitation and welcome. Babies cannot force their way to the breast; they have no power to command—only the power to ask when in need. To be seen and perceived by another in our need and our desire and to have that seeing give birth to an invitation is so very powerful. Come close, child. Come rest here. Be satisfied at my breast. Be welcome close to my heart. Stay as long as you need, as long as it takes to be soothed in body and soul. I will hold you, cover you with my own body. You are loved.

The mercy culture of the womb offers compassion and forgiveness. Mercy's message is that we are loved for who we are and that we are rescued from the mistakes we make—rescued from willful disobedience, from misguided independence, from sin. Mercy offers compassion, seeing us in our frailty and our glory. The assurance of abundance speaks that mercy will never run out and will always be greater than our waywardness. Assurance of abundance allows us to live from desire and not just need. There is more than enough provision in Mother's breasts. We don't have to worry or fret or scheme about how to provide for ourselves or how to obtain the forgiveness we will surely need.

King David also speaks to the emotional benefits when he uses the metaphor of a child held against his mother's breast in Psalm 131:2 (GNT),

> Instead, I am content and at peace.
> As a child lies quietly in its mother's arms,
> so my heart is quiet within me.

The idea here is of one who is settled of heart and resting in contentment and solace. Is it any wonder then that so many soldiers, as they die on the battlefield, call out for their mothers? Or that we, in our deep adult distress, feel again like a child longing for her home in her mother's embrace.

In *Essay for Good Friday*, Sarah Bessey writes of her daughter, "And so when she wakes up or when she's lonely or when she's hungry or just wants someone to hold her, to calm her heart, she cries out and I quickly come to her, I rush to her, and I lift her up into my arms, *shhhh, I'm here, you're not alone, I'm here, I've got you, I've got you,* I say**.** Oh, I'm teaching her something: I'm teaching her that I will always come for her. I'm teaching her that she is safe and secure. I'm teaching her that I am reliable, that she is believed, that I don't believe she's manipulating me or bossing me. I'm teaching my child that I am here and she is not alone. Dry your tears, small girl, I'm here, I'm always here. I will always come for you."[5]

We are never too old, never too adult for those words. My best friend Melissa has just lost her mother to a wicked and fast-progressing dementia. Never mind that Melissa is a fully grown and functional adult. Even so, it is a devastating prospect to lose the mother who has always been there, who has come for her over and over, and who has been a haven of safety in the midst of life's hardships. Some of you have lost mothers in this way, to death. Others of you lost what is in *mother* before you could ever experience it. Perhaps you've never known what Amma, El Shaddai intended you to experience in the arms of an earthly mother who was meant to echo the heart of

---

[5] . I'm Here, You're not Alone: Essay for Good Friday from Sarah Bessey's Field Notes, 2022, by Sarah Bessey, https://sarahbessey.substack.com/p/good-friday.

heaven. You were meant to have that but didn't for the myriad of reasons that might have been. Perhaps your mother was herself motherless as a child and could not give you what she never had. Perhaps she lost herself along the way in hardship, from mistreatment, through addiction, or the mishandling of her own heart. It might be easy to blame her, hate her, shove her away even as you long for her to show up better for you even now. What happened to you isn't OK. But you can return to El Shaddai who will always extend Her heart to you. And you can choose to see your earthly mother in her little girl woundedness and her adult woman inadequacies and remember that your own breasts can offer her compassion and mercy even when it is undeserved.

What is in the name of El Shaddai? The Trinity's offer and great desire to nourish our lives from a place of Their own abundance. Many years ago now, I was in a conversation with God over the medical crisis of one of my cats. This cat in particular held my heart's affection, and we had been through much together. As I was talking with God about healing my sweet fur baby, I was declaring all that I knew about Jesus and healing. How His suffering had purchased that for us. How Father's commitment to healing us was manifested in the ministry of Jesus who never turned away or put off till later a person who approached him for healing. I reminded myself of the Sun of Righteousness that rises with healing in His wings (Malachi 4:2). As I was speaking, there was this moment when I heard the Trinity say that not only could I have all that is Theirs, but I could also have all that They *are*. Do you know how much that is? How much abundance is in the Trinity? All the love and kindness and mercy and compassion, the faithfulness and strength, and wisdom and truth. The offer is that you and I, dear daughter, can drink to our heart's content of all of God. El Shaddai holds back no good thing from us. Her invitation is that we come and drink until we are satisfied and at rest.

Restful babies aren't just restful because their bellies are

She

full. They are calmed by their mother's warmth and stillness. The beauty of her face captures their attention; her softness invites them to rest. Babies have no sense of being small and vulnerable as they rest against their mothers. Instead, they see themselves as one with her, protected in her. This too is part of El Shaddai's invitation to us—to lose ourselves in Her beauty, to be quieted by Her tenderness, and to trust Her to guard our lives.

We cannot offer these things to others until we first receive them from God. And oh, how we need to receive them. Women tend to be what hold families together—the center of the wheel—and so we are busy creatures. Much of our lives is spent on others, making their lives possible and making life run smoothly. Read the description of the woman in Proverbs 31. The poor woman barely sleeps. We are no different today. Life is full and much pulls at us. Women are notoriously bad at taking care of themselves. The truth is that while the occasional pedicure is lovely, my soul needs more than that. I need a soft place to land where I can hand over to someone else the weight that I carry. I need to be still. My soul needs to rest. I need El Shaddai.

The need to be safe in rest is related to our need for comfort, for the tending of our distress by meeting our needs both emotional and physical. Here again, we find Mother God. Allow me to give you some context. The name Jerusalem is a compound of two words. The first means *they see and in seeing, they provide.* The second word is peace—being whole and without injury. Taken together, Jerusalem means "They [the Trinity] see us and in Their seeing provide for our peace—our wholeness, to heal us from injury." This is why Zechariah tells us that God dwells in Jerusalem. In Isaiah 66:11–13 (NIV), God speaks of Jerusalem as the place where we will find the presence and therefore the comfort of El Shaddai:

> For you will nurse and be satisfied at her [Jerusalem's] comforting breasts; you will drink deeply and delight in her overflowing abundance." For this is what the LORD says: "I will extend peace to her like a river, and the wealth of nations like a flooding stream; you will nurse and be carried on her arm and dandled on her knees. As a mother comforts her child, so will I comfort you.

When was the last time you were comforted? The last time someone gathered you into their arms and made it safe for you to express your distress? Have you ever felt more whole after receiving comfort? This is the promise of El Shaddai—that if we come to Her in our sadness and grief, in the rending of our hearts, and in the weight of life and the exhaustion from carrying it, She will bring us up onto Her lap and comfort us with Her tenderness and kindness. She will see us, truly see us, and not push away our distress, call it invalid, or explain it away. But She will let us pour out our angst and in response will dry our tears and make peace for our souls. *Selah.*

> *Amma, Mama God, El Shaddai, I know You see the places of my sadness and grief. The weighty angst I have tucked away from sight. I don't have to explain it to You. You know. You know. And You will love me past my pain, putting together the pieces of my broken heart.*

Another aspect of the Trinity that is stunningly beautiful in its expression through Mother God is Her unconditional love for us. She loves us because we came from Her; She bore us. We are the children Her heart longed for because we were created in love and for love. There is no performance demand in that. Whether we stand in moments of glorious accomplishment or show up as a hot mess, we are welcomed into Her embrace and given a place at Her table. Amma finds us lovely whether or not we feel that way. Being in a relationship with God who sees us clearly and fully and does not blink at our failures or our wandering progress conveys the message that all will be well. It's going to be OK. *We* are going to be OK. Mothers have such a rare capacity to help us feel that.

In a post-Eden world where sin has taken its toll and humanity lives far from the glory of our design, having a God who can and will make all things right and new is a treasure that defies words. Most of us (dare I say, *all*?) experience significant father and mother wounds. That is the inevitable consequence of the human choice to abandon God as Father and Mother. We have cut ourselves off from receiving the parenting of God, and we have also lost the benefit of having the Trinity as a model for our own parenting. Though the vast majority of parents intend good for their children, the ability to walk well in that is compromised by the wounds of their own hearts.

Poor attachment is generally referred to as mother deprivation, but Eldredge has coined what I think is a better term—*mother desolation*. It isn't just that people might be deprived or lacking in attachment with their mothers. It's that the lack produces soul desolation—emptiness, ruin, deep grief, and loneliness. Desolation is a word that implies a barrenness of terrain where things have trouble growing.

This is what happens when we grow up without consistent exposure to the face of love and to the nurturing breast. Our hearts are starved; there isn't enough emotional nourishment for us to properly develop. And we are left feeling *less than* and *not enough*. There is a core wound to our sense of safety, worth, and belonging. This is why we need El Shaddai. She is the only Mother who is enough to heal us.

Amma, El Shaddai, we run into Your arms, into Your invitation to receive Your love. We bring with us the barrenness of our hearts and the painful questions that have haunted us about our worth. We long to find our home in You, safe haven, belonging, nurture, abundance, comfort, and unconditional affection. Restore us, Amma. Let us be children again in Your care so that we know You as our true Mother and as our beginning place.

Chapter 4

The Apple and the Tree

Your heart itself, as a woman, is an invitation...Your Lover has written something on your heart.
It is a call to find a life of Romance and to protect that love affair as your most precious treasure. A call to cultivate the beauty you hold inside, and to unveil your beauty on behalf of others. And it is a call to adventure, to become the *ezer* the world desperately needs you to be.
—John and Stasi Eldredge, *Captivating*

What does it mean to be a woman? To possess and embody femininity? I'm hesitant to even use that word as it has become laden with all sorts of meaning, much of it errant, and some of it abusive. To be clear, when I speak of the feminine soul, I'm simply referring to a commonality that comes from the biology, psychology, and spirituality of being female. I also want to be clear that femininity comes in many shapes and sizes. Not all women are alike, any more than all men are alike. Yet we have the two essential groups because "male and female, God created them." But more importantly, the Trinity created us in Their image, so the answer to "What does it mean to be a woman?" begins with another question, "What is the Trinity representing of themselves *through women*?" Regardless of how we feel about the matter, the truth is that there is a blueprint for the feminine soul and it is an echo of Amma/El Shaddai/Ruach HaKodesh. It isn't just that the apple doesn't fall far from the tree, but that the apple takes on the character of the tree that produced it. This is the truth again that identity flows from attachment relationships.

Beauty

> Beauty is one of the most mysterious and misunderstood realities in life. Of course it is—beauty entices our hearts back, and beyond. It beckons us back to the original intent … and beyond to a place which transcends the mess. (Jan Meyers)

> Here's the one thing I crave from Yahweh, the one thing I seek above all else: I want to live with him every moment in his house, beholding the marvelous beauty of Yahweh, filled with awe, delighting in his glory and grace. (Psalm 27:4 TPT)

God is beautiful. We don't think about that so much in this day and age since we tend to view God as a disembodied ethereal spirit. But once upon a time, before the great ruining, the Trinity walked on the earth—face-to-face with Their children. Adam and Eve encountered the Trinity with all five of their senses. And in the space beyond time, God also has *physical substance*—at least in the sense that the Trinity can be seen and heard and felt. We see it in Jesus being transfigured into the glory of His Godhood on the Mount of Olives. And we know this because there are multiple descriptions in scripture

She

of people being taken in the spirit up to heaven where they encountered the presence of God and could describe that in sound and visual images. For example,

Your eyes will see the King in His beauty. (Isaiah 33:17 AMP)

> Then as I looked, I saw a door standing open in heaven, and the same voice I had heard before, which sounded like a mighty trumpet blast, spoke to me and said, "Come up here and I will show you what must happen in the future!" And instantly I was in spirit there in heaven and saw—oh, the glory of it!—a throne and someone sitting on it! Great bursts of light flashed forth from him as from a glittering diamond or from a shining ruby, and a rainbow glowing like an emerald encircled his throne. (Revelation 4:1–3 TLB)

Another way we encounter the beauty of God is through creation. Understand that no created thing originated in itself. Beauty does not exist outside of God or apart from God any more than does love or holiness or life. All are a reflection of the One Who made them.

> For since the creation of the world His invisible attributes, His eternal power and divine nature, *have been clearly seen, being understood through what has been made,* so that they are without excuse. (Romans 1:20, emphasis mine)

John Eldredge makes the observation that when you read the creation story in Genesis, you see a progression of complexity, wonder, and beauty. Like music that swells to crescendo, like a painting—created in layers until it culminates into a focal point: humanity, made not just *by* God but *in the image of God.* Each of the elements of creation speaks to the attributes of the Trinity, but it is here, on the sixth day, that God is most clearly revealed. Since the woman is the final act of creation, that leads Eldredge to say that "Eve is the crown of creation, remember? She embodies the exquisite beauty and the exotic mystery of God in a way that nothing else in all creation even comes close to."[6]

This is why Stasi Eldredge writes, "Beauty is transcendent. It is our most immediate experience of the eternal. Think of what it's like to behold a gorgeous sunset or the ocean at dawn. Remember the ending of a great story. We yearn to linger, to experience it all our days. Sometimes the beauty is so deep it pierces us with longing. For what? For life as it was meant to be. Beauty reminds us of an Eden we have never known, but somehow our hearts were created for."[7]

Before we go any further, I want to clarify what I mean and what is meant scripturally by the concept of beauty. This is anything—external or internal—that draws another to us in a way that is satisfying and pleasing. Even more strongly, the Hebrew word for beauty suggests something that is radiant, creating a sense of awe and wonder and being special and unique.

Beauty is probably best understood from the effects it has. Think back on what you experience, feel, and think when you encounter beauty. It doesn't matter what the source is— whether a flower, a person, an animal, the mountains, or a burning bush. Beauty has this quality of wonder and delight that causes us to stop what we're doing. It invites us to enter in, to move into it, and to be still so that beauty can speak to our souls. And if we do that, if we come away into beauty's presence, some metaphysical thing happens where we are

---

[6] . Wild at Heart: Discovering the Secret of a Man's Soul, Thomas Nelson Publishers 2010, by John Eldredge

[7] . Captivating: Unveiling the Mystery of a Woman's Soul, Thomas Nelson Publishers (2007), by John & Stasi Eldredge

surrounded by its essence and held inside of it in a way that allows beauty to also enter us. It begins to stir something in us—something emotional and often beyond words. It loosens our clenched jaws and knotted muscles. It releases our hearts; there is a letting go that is possible when we are held by beauty. In its caress, there is healing for our souls. Anxiety drops away, along with its other friends—stress, panic, grief, trauma, and loneliness.

When speaking of beauty in the context of people (and the Trinity), there is a relationship between internal and external beauty. For example, one of the quickest ways to diminish external beauty is to pair it with an ugly spirit—one characterized by bitterness, anger, greed, grasping, insecurity, and the like. This is true whether we're speaking of women or men. And the opposite is also true, that physical appearance is made even more beautiful by the internal beauty which shines through it.

OK, so let's be real here. Beauty is one of the most assaulted concepts in the life of women. For most of us, probably all of us, it is a cause of pain at some level. The pain comes from a variety of sources. Most of us have had our beauty denied at some point—burnt up in the fires of rejection or comparison and their accompanying message that our beauty is not enough. That message comes from individual people in our lives as well as an industry that claims to hold the standards for it.

Is beauty in the eye of the beholder as the saying goes? If it is, then beauty is entirely subjective. However, we're talking here about people *as a reflection of God* whose qualities do not change based on others' opinions. For example, God is faithful no matter how it might appear. The Trinity is kind even in the face of suffering and holy even when earthly standards of integrity change. It only makes sense then that God's beauty, and by extension, our beauty is factual—an objective Truth that doesn't depend on the agreement of anyone or anything. Because you were made in the image of the One who has indisputable worth, it must also be part of your DNA. And that, dear daughter, must mean that you also have a beauty that is beyond question. I realize that that doesn't match much of our experience and so most of us struggle with feeling that truth even if our heads are willing to accept it.

I remember clearly the first assault on my sense of beauty. I was eight or nine—long before boys entered the picture. As I was playing with two friends who lived across the street, for whatever reason, the subject of weight came up and each of them (tiny little waifs that they were) announced what their scale had told them. So I answered as well. There were gasps and incredulous looks. And the words "you weigh how much?" Mind you, I was a normal-weight child though always on the tall side. Up to that moment, I had never considered the issue of weight for myself. But in the span of seconds, that all changed, replaced by a conscious belief that I was fat and that it should be a matter of embarrassment.

The newly born belief wasn't just a cognitive thought but an emotional one. I know this because in the years that followed, that perception of myself endured no matter what the scales said. It wasn't until forty(!) years later when I stumbled across an old photo album and thumbed through its pages that I realized my perception was wrong. Wrong. There was proof in photo after photo of the little girl I was—not fat, not an embarrassment, not anything but lovely. That realization broke my heart. I had believed a lie for so many years, and it had mattered.

I want to be clear about something. The lie that entered my heart that day wasn't just about the neighbor children's interpretation of my weight. More importantly, the lie was that beauty was determined by weight. This began the season of embracing the lie that beauty is subjective. There would be later additions to the lie, which came in adolescence, then again in adulthood, in messages from boys, and then men. Additions that would pile on other requirements to beauty, the totality of which was unachievable. The requirements were also false, but I didn't know that then so I allowed those to torment my heart as well.

What has your relationship with beauty been like? What have you believed about yourself? What are the sources of diminishment or disqualification you've encountered? Where in your story did someone cause you to doubt that you possess a beauty that is beyond question?

We are our most beautiful when we believe that we are loved.
—Stasi Eldredge

Perhaps part of our difficulty comes from wearing the wrong lenses. You've probably heard the phrase, "They've got a face only their mother could love." The suggestion here is that mothers are biased to see their children as lovely even if they aren't. But what if it isn't a matter of bias but rather a moment of clarity that comes from looking through the lens of Love? What if Love is the only way to see the Truth of beauty, and all other seeing only reveals truth with a little *t*—the eye-of-the-beholder kind of truth? This would explain a lot. Like for example, the way people look more beautiful to us the more we love them. And how the loss of love causes us to focus on flaws and ugliness. What is the lens through which you look at yourself? Is it critical? Is it full of impossible standards and expectations? Is it a lens of shame and remembered failure, a lens of comparison? Or is it a mother's lens of grace and mercy, compassion, and love?

> *Amma, El Shaddai, what do You see when You look at me with Your Mother's heart of love? What is the beauty I possess? Help me please to see it and myself as You do. And Ruach HaKodesh, bring to light every false lens, every false word of accusation that has come against my beauty. Burn away my pain in the light of Your truth. Root*

> *out the lies and lead me in the forgiveness of those who spoke them.*

We must also receive God's grace for the ways in which we may have marred or obscured our own beauty. For example, in the story of the prodigal son, the depth of his rebellion leads him to a place where he is literally covered in pig slop. That is how far he has fallen from the truth of his identity as a beloved son. And he has done this to his own soul—this is not a wounding from another's words but rather his choice to embrace pursuits that did not lead to life. This serves as a lesson in another truth about identity:

> Because we are made in the likeness of God, we must continue to live in the culture, company, and environment of God in order to be whole and without injury.

When you take something and remove it from the environment that gives it life, you can expect death or at the very least, some sort of tarnishing or decay. For example, a fish, which is not made to exist on dry land, will die outside of water. Iron, which is not made to exist in water, will corrode unless it is coated in a protective barrier. Your heart, your soul, your body, your mind, and *your beauty* all require us to be tethered to God in intimacy and relationship. It is the relationship of fruit to the vine. Apart from the vine, it shrivels and dies. This is why we need to come to God for restoration, reconnection, and forgiveness for the ways that we have marred our own beauty or covered it over in pig slop by disconnecting it from its life source.

This includes how beauty is used. It is meant to be offered for the good of the other—to draw them into a multitude of graces and to reflect God. But sometimes we offer our beauty out of more manipulative motives, using it as a tool or a means to an end. I'm speaking here both of physical beauty as well as emotional, spiritual, and relational beauty. There's a fine line to be walked here. Some but not all appeals based on physical or relational beauty are manipulative. The line seems to be determined by two questions. The first is whether we're offering our beauty for another's good or offering in order to get something from them. The latter brings up the possibility that what we are trying to get is something the other person might not willingly offer without our efforts. For example, in the context of a *healthy* marriage where two people are living in emotional intimacy and loving each other well, dressing for your husband in a way that you know pleases and stirs him is not manipulative. But to offer your beauty in order to draw someone into a relationship when they don't want to be or to offer sex to someone who is not your husband in order to gain their favor or keep them in a relationship is manipulative.

Genesis 3:6 records the moment when Eve crossed this line with Adam. She had already chosen to engage in unbelief and accusation against Father, and then she goes to Adam and invites him to join her. Understand that this is Eve, using her beauty and the beauty inherent in her relationship value to Adam to get him to choose her over the Trinity. This is not for Adam's good. It isn't motivated by love. Rather it seems to be about Eve not wanting to be alone in her choice and in the consequences that would flow from it.

This moment set up a dynamic that will haunt women for the rest of time. It caused Adam and all of his sons after him to be caught between being drawn to Eve's beauty (rightfully so) and being suspicious and afraid of it (understandably so). It is what has spawned years of usually unfair accusations in the workplace that women advance in their jobs because of their beauty rather than their skill and competence. While this is not true of most successful women, the fact that some women use their beauty in this way only serves to give fuel to the mistrust that dates to Eden.

Sometimes the unhealthy offering of our beauty is an

attempt to get validation that we do in fact possess beauty. Because we've understood it very poorly, beauty has become synonymous in our culture with perfection according to some arbitrary and unattainable physical standard. We live in a world of such artificiality that even photos of supermodels are airbrushed to eliminate "flaws". It is sheer insanity. In that climate, insecurity is a given. I so appreciate Stasi Eldredge's thoughts on the subject. She says that we are most beautiful when

> We are not trying to obtain it.
> We are not doubting that we possess it.
> We are not looking to others to validate it.
> But we are simply resting in it.

To do this—to rest in the certainty that we possess a beauty, that cannot be taken or lost, requires a heart that has met redemption, a heart that knows, that it knows that it is well-loved and wanted. Remember that love is required to make visible what is lovely. Love is what reveals beauty's presence. The question over your life should never be *whether* you have a beauty that is all your own. You do. It is part of how you reflect the Trinity in the essence of your femininity. The problem is that others (and maybe even you) may not have the ability to perceive it because their eyes are not rooted in the Truth of Love. Until we understand ourselves as being created by Love, created in the likeness of the Trinity (more specifically, the likeness of El Shaddai and Ruach HaKodesh), and born with internal and external beauty that is factual rather than a matter of opinion, our souls will not be at rest on this issue.

If your heart struggles to come into this Truth of you, let me suggest something that might help. Although there are feelings and emotions that flow from and are connected to Truth, Truth is more than just feelings. It is a heart-mind conviction—a belief, that brings us into an agreement with what God has said. So rather than expecting your heart to be able to feel beautiful right from the start, it will probably be important to begin with the choice to believe God regardless of how you feel. This is an aspect of spiritual warfare that is common in life with God. And it is the part where Eve struggles.

Second Corinthians 10:5 gives us the *how* of this: *Take thoughts captive in obedience to Jesus.* This involves you taking a stand against every lie that accuses your beauty—calling it a lie and then binding it to the truth that is in Christ. Then the additional strategy comes from Luke 11:24–26 which tells us to replace lies with Truth, or else the lies will come back to occupy the empty space. This is echoed in Philippians 4:8, which tells us to think on what is good and lovely and true. In this case, the truth is that you've been created to be beautiful (e.g., Genesis 1:27, 31; Psalm 139:14; Song of Songs 4:1, 7). Spend some time receiving the voice and heart of Jesus, the Divine Husband as He speaks in the Song of Songs 1:15 (TPT),

My darling, you are so lovely! You are beauty itself to me.

If you will begin here, in the battle for the mind and for your belief in what God says, then the feelings will eventually come in line. It is also important to forgive others and yourself for all the ways in which your beauty has been assaulted.

> *Abba Father, Amma Mother, Jesus—Lover of my soul, Ruach HaKodesh, I invite You into this battle over my beauty. Give me discernment over the lies I have believed; help me to be honest about the pain I feel from the wounds I have been dealt. Let Your love for me wash over these embattled places and reveal my beauty. Bring me to rest about it. Cleanse my mind and heart from all the false standards and judgments I've accepted and lead me in breaking agreements I've made that disparage my beauty. I come into*

> *agreement that You who are beautiful, You who define beauty—You have called me beautiful, lovely, wanted, and adored. I receive that as truth and speak it over myself.*

Another aspect of God's loveliness is that the Trinity rests. God is not anxious or fretful, never scurrying about or panicking even when there is urgency. We see Jesus in the boat in the midst of a storm so terrible that seasoned fishermen are panicking. And He's asleep! Or consider the urgency that comes when Eden falls and now the fate of all of creation hinges on a series of people throughout time which will ultimately culminate in Jesus. Even then, when the story could go awry at any moment, God rests. It is the rest of One who is wholly Other, who stands beyond time and sees and knows everything that will be. They are a Trinity whose very essence holds all things together and who is well able to bring to a finish the plan They have set in motion to make all things good. This is an echo of the Trinity creating the world. Then the very next thing we hear in Genesis is that God rested.

This explains why we're so drawn to things at rest like sleeping babies or animals. The peace (wholeness) that allows them to rest is beautiful, and it captures our hearts' attention. We turn aside to watch, and in that moment, we are drawn into rest. Rest is beautiful, and beauty invites us to rest. I love the picture of this in Song of Songs 4 (TPT) where the male lover is celebrating his beloved's beauty. In verses 9–15, there are these descriptions of the interplay between her internal and external beauty and the effect it has on him:

> For you reach into my heart. With one flash of your eyes I am undone by your love, my beloved, my equal, my bride. You leave me breathless—I am overcome by merely a glance from your worshiping eyes, for you have stolen my heart. I

> am held hostage by your love and by the graces of righteousness shining upon you. My darling bride, my private paradise, fastened to my heart. A secret spring that no one else can have are you—my bubbling fountain hidden from public view ... inward life is now sprouting, bringing forth fruit ... What a beautiful paradise unfolds within you ... You are a fountain of gardens. A well of living water springs up from within you, like a mountain brook flowing into my heart!

Then in verse 16, the bride responds to these words with an invitation:

> Awake, O north wind! Awake, O south wind! Breathe on my garden with your Spirit-Wind. Stir up the sweet spice of your life within me. Spare nothing as you make me your fruitful garden. Hold nothing back until I release your fragrance. *Come walk with me as you walked with Adam* in your paradise garden. *Come taste the fruits of your life in me.*

This invitation to come in and to walk with her is an invitation to rest. In effect, she says "Come aside from everything else that's on your mind and be lost in my beauty. Be soothed by it, take comfort in it, let it nourish your soul." This is what the Spirit of God whispers to our souls. And this, dear daughter, is what your life can offer as you become settled in your beauty and live connected to the Holy Spirit, Ruach HaKodesh, Who will breathe on you to stir up the life of God within you. From that secure place of knowing God and knowing your worth, your very entrance into a room serves as an invitation to all present there, "Come away and rest in knowing that all will be well, all will be good."

Made for an Intimate Relationship

We've already talked a bit about the relational nature of the Trinity, our three-in-one God. We've looked at the moment when Father explained to Adam that human design requires a relationship with others of like kind; the animals were not enough. It wasn't good for Adam to be alone, and that wasn't because he was a man. It was because he was human. God's statement to Adam is about all of us, so women start with a similar truth. We are made for intimate relationships.

This begins in union with God. Remember you were designed and created out of the Trinity's love for one another—created by Their love, for Their love. You, daughter, are the object of Their delight.

> For you created my inmost being; you knit me together in my mother's womb. I praise you because I am fearfully and wonderfully made; your works are wonderful, I know that full well. My frame was not hidden from you when I was made in the secret place, when I was woven together in the depths of the earth. Your eyes saw my unformed body; the days ordained for me were written in your book before one of them came to be. (Psalm 139:13–16 NIV)

Our lives begin in this context, the intimate act of creation when you were uniquely designed and handcrafted. You were made with purpose and forethought, made from desire and longing. Your life represents the goodness of God poured into the frame of your existence. You are a delight to the Trinity who is intimately acquainted with all of your being and more specifically, to Father and Mother God who are your beginning.

Part of the design of women is to represent within marriage the mature love found in a one-flesh union since the ultimate destiny of humankind is to be the bride of Christ. In this sense, we exist as brides and as wives on the earth to help provide a tangible model for what will be true at the end of the age. Toward that end, we are designed with unique beauty of form and spirit. We were meant to be fearless in love and courageous in leaning into the Lover of our souls because our time with Him has taught us to trust Him. Women are meant to lead the way in modeling that courageous vulnerability and transparency. It takes tremendous security of identity and soundness of heart to be able to join ourselves to another without losing who we are in the process.

When things are well with our souls, we can offer ourselves to others wholeheartedly from a place of free choice without restraint or hindrance. There is liberty to be generous with what our hearts have, in love, been given. There is this remarkable opportunity as women to be loved by God, and then, in turn, pour that love back onto Him. This is the circle of love which is without end, each pouring onto the other in increasing generosity and intimacy.

Since connectedness through relationship is a core value and Truth of the Trinity, and since we are patterned after them, it follows that Eve and her daughters are designed for relationships with people as are Adam and his sons. It must be equally true of both genders despite some of our cultural beliefs. Relationships don't work when one party is more suited or drawn to connectedness and intimacy than another. That kind of inequality produces a dynamic where one person is usually the pursuer and sacrificer and the other acts either in retreat or indifference. The kind of union and intimacy that the Trinity exhibits within Themselves and which they intended for us depends on both parties deeply valuing union and intimacy—each playing love's role of pursuer and sacrificer.

Genesis 2:18–23 records God's explanation of humanity's relational design. The emphasis in what God reveals here is the issue of the not-goodness of being alone. Now obviously, God was not speaking literally about aloneness since Adam stood there in the company of the Trinity and all of the other created things. I have a special appreciation for this last part as I have spent my entire life in the company of animals. I've enjoyed their companionship—the funny games that Little Miss Buttons thinks up for the two of us to play. And the intense desire my Great Danes have to be with me in all of my life's activities from cooking to meeting with clients to brushing my teeth. (In case you've never lived with a Great Dane, let me just tell you that you're *never* alone if they have anything to say about it). I cannot imagine life without furry things, yet for all of their charms, they are not *like me*. This is the essential need that Father speaks to with Adam. Something about the human soul needs a relationship with another complementary human soul.

Adam needs an explicit explanation of this by Father because he was "born" into an environment in which he was the only one of his kind. In the kindness of progressive revelation, Father teaches Adam about himself, about his design, and the relational need that flows from it. Eve's experience was a bit different. She was "born" into a world where Adam already existed, which means that she was born into a relationship. This was her original norm. Scripture records Adam's revelatory moment where he recognizes that Eve is "bone of my bone, and flesh of my flesh." The realization that she is like him and made from him, leads Adam to a startling conclusion—the two of them are actually part of one whole. This is another way in which people reflect the Trinity.

I can't help but wonder if the difference in Adam and Eve's beginnings continues to be reflected in the generations born from them. Could it be true that what came naturally to Eve, her being born into a relationship, is passed to her daughters and reflected in the deep heart pull we feel toward intimacy and oneness? And if so, could it also be true that like Adam, men are more likely to need an explicit revelation of that? This would explain some things. For example, culturally, we tend to portray women as being more relational than men and more *wired* for relationship. I don't think that can be true from a scriptural perspective but what if women are more intuitively *aware* of their relational needs and design—a gap that seems to get widened after the fall of Eden?

Despite the fact that both men and women are made for intimacy, there are likely differences between the two genders surrounding what we look like in relationships and how we show up for people in our lives. Some of this is reflected in biological differences the Trinity wove into our design. For example, generally speaking, the part of the brain responsible for language tends to be better developed in women and is better connected to the rest of the brain (including emotional centers). You know where I'm headed with this. Yep, we tend to talk. About everything. Even if only to ourselves. Women tend to process the world and their experiences in words, so we value conversation. This feels like intimacy to us since we are better able to express our emotions verbally. For many men, intimacy is more easily found in shared adventure and activity. Get men doing something (especially driving a car), and you'll find them more receptive to talking.

Out of the mother heart of El Shaddai, women tend to take very nurturing positions in their relationships. The same half of the brain that specializes in language also specializes in details and that shows up in how we offer care, support, and encouragement. Often through our words, but not only through words, we cause others to feel seen and met by noticing the details of their lives. We ask for the details. This is part of how we offer warmth and compassion. On an interesting note, around moral issues, there are studies, which suggest that women—more than men—tend to make moral decisions by paying attention to the other person's context and issues that might mediate their behavior. This is called care-based reasoning.

Lenne' Hunt

Intimate Allies

Practically speaking, the first view we have of Eve in relationship with people is in her life with Adam. But the relationship with Adam might be a bit different than you've been led to believe. So many of the women I journey with come to me after having experienced years of exposure to a theology of women which emphasizes submission and subordination as the defining attributes of femininity. Perhaps you've come from a similar background. It is worth spending a few words to address this.

In Genesis, the Trinity gives us two clear and defining descriptors of Eve and her daughters. First, they must be like Adam. Remember the animals weren't enough. Father told Adam that he needed another *like himself*. This is reflected in God's use of the word *kenegdo*, which only occurs here in the creation of Eve. It is generally translated as opposite (in the sense that Eve stands in front of Adam, face-to-face with him), similar, and corresponding. There is nothing in this word *kenegdo* to suggest submission or subordination.

In affirming the idea of *similarity* and *correspondence*, Marg Mowczk writes that Adam's understanding of similarity is seen in his "description of the first woman who was formed from a side or part taken out of his own body: 'This is now bone of my bones, and flesh of my flesh' (Genesis 2:23)". The man noticed the similarities, that they had the same nature, that the woman was his "counterpart, complement, companion and partner."[8] Brad Gray of *Walking the Text*, adds that "when understood holistically, and in its proper context, kenegdo means 'one who stands in front of or opposite to.' It's the idea of someone who stands before you, facing you, opposing you, not simply allowing you to go whichever direction you choose. It's a word

---
[8] . Kenegdo: Is the woman subordinate, suitable, or similar to the man?, 2014 by Marg Mowczk, https://margmowczko.com/kenegdo-meet-subordinate-suitable-or-similar/

picture for how one is to relate to another. In more practical terms, we could say a kenegdo is someone who questions, confronts, challenges, and holds another accountable."

The second descriptor Father gave to Adam explains why Eve is to be his equal and similar partner. This is the word *ezer* which means to aid, rescue, save; to be strong. It is a term used consistently in scripture in the context of battle, referring to an equal or superior who lends aid or comes to defend. Most often, it is a reference to God as our savior and rescuer.

When we put the two descriptors together as the Trinity does in the creation story, we get *ezer kenegdo*, an equal partner who joins Adam as a trusted ally and who has the strength, power, resources, and ability to help in times of battle. Eve is a *warrior*! She was born with a sword in her hand and fierceness in her heart. This should actually come as no surprise if we remember the relationship between the apple and the tree. Eve is patterned after the Trinity, and Exodus 15:3 tells us that the Lord is a warrior. More specifically, Eve is patterned after El Shaddai. Have you ever met a mama bear with her cubs? Heaven help you if you do. Mother God is tender and compassionate, and She is also fierce and protective of those She loves, those She has birthed and nurtured. Nobody harms Her babies!

> God has spoken once, Twice I have heard this:
> That power belongs to God. Also to You, O Lord,
> belong lovingkindness and compassion. (Psalm 62:11–12 AMP)

This is woman, patterned after God—woman, who has a womb of compassion and who is strong to rescue and defend.

After discovering for herself that God created women to be strong and valiant warriors, Carolyn Custis James writes, "That night, while the rest of the world slept, my identity changed forever. I couldn't think of a single moment, situation or relationship in my life where my calling as an *ezer*-warrior for God's purposes didn't apply."[9] You see, Eve wasn't an ezer just for Adam. She acted as an ezer throughout her life because that is who she was by nature.

> *Holy Spirit, Ruach HaKodesh, I need You to cleanse my understanding of myself. Strip away the lies I have believed and illuminate the truth that has been hidden from me. Teach me to find my strength in You so that I can turn around and offer that strength to those who are besieged and under fire. But let my strength be tempered and harnessed by compassion and lovingkindness and accompanied by the wisdom to know when to employ both parts of myself.*

The Ultimate Battle

I want to take you back to the moment when Father introduced to Adam the idea of an ezer kenegdo. Remember that the context is Eden, perfect Eden. Imagine that you're Adam and have just heard God say, "Adam, you're going to need a strong ally who will fight back to back with you in battle." Scripture doesn't record Adam's response, but I imagine it sounded something like this, "Huh? What's a battle and why do I need an ally?" You get it, right? Adam has no context for what Father has just told him. As far as Adam knows, life will consist of adventuring in the garden with the Trinity (and whoever this new person is whom God is bringing) as they push the boundaries of Eden forward until it covers the whole earth. He knows nothing of battle, nothing of an enemy. But Father knows. Heaven has already endured the great betrayal and rebellion led by Lucifer. And Father knows that the former angel of light is going to take aim at what the Trinity loves most, humankind.

---

[9] . The Return of the Ezer, Missio Alliance (2005), by Carolyn Custis James

She

Now here is where the story gets *really* interesting. The wily snake decides to target Eve. Why Eve? Many would say it was because she was the weaker of the two. Though that may have been true physically, this was not going to be a physical battle, but even if it was, the Trinity made her to be a skilled warrior. Also there is nothing in scripture to support that Eve was weaker than Adam spiritually or psychologically. So again, I ask, Why Eve?

The answer seems to be found in Lucifer's jealousy and his quest to regain what he'd lost. Ezekiel 28:11–14 (AMP) describes Lucifer (before his fall) as full of wisdom and perfect in beauty, "the anointed cherub who covers and protects." Aside from the cherub part, the qualities listed there could also be applied to Eve. Wisdom is represented in scripture as a *she*. Beauty is an aspect of the feminine. "Covers and protects" is in line with being an ezer. Add to that an issue that applies equally to Adam and Eve as children of God and not merely angels—they are joint heirs with Christ to the throne of God. This was the thing Lucifer desired most of all. In the end, Eve represents all that Lucifer grabbed for in his rebellion against God. Now was his chance to bring down the rightful heir to those things.

This begins a tale of woe that has stalked the feminine soul from the fall of Eden onward. Unfortunately, Satan's jealousy of and hatred toward Eve doesn't stop with Eden. This is an assault, which stretches across all time. I expect there are elements in your story, which testify to that. Across time and culture and geography, there is a malice toward women that has raged since this moment in the garden. Certainly, Satan comes after men too; that is its own tale of woe. But the assault on women is several notches up on the scale of evil. It has taken many forms over the centuries from viewing women as property to sanctioning marital rape. It has been manifested in binding feet to keep them small (and in the process, causing unimaginable pain and severe physical impairment), in taking away women's voice in government, and in paying them less than men for doing the same jobs. It is played out in the forced removal of the clitoris and in withholding education. We see it in much of Christendom as well, where the misunderstood concept of submission has been mistakenly used as a means of control. As Adam blamed Eve ("this woman you gave me" in Genesis 3:12), this has often been the basis for viewing her as more responsible for the fall of humankind (and therefore more suspect in her character). Misogyny touches all aspects of life.

Does this help to make sense of your own story? When viewed through this lens, are you able to see that much of what has been brought against you is authored by the kingdom of darkness? This is a hard truth about what it means to be a woman. We are, by our essence, Satan's enemy and the object of his hatred. Where have you experienced this in your own story? What are the ways in which you've been opposed or made to feel less than because you are a woman? Whose voices have spoken such things to your heart? From what source(s) have you experienced violence against your femininity?

> *Holy Spirit, Ruach HaKodesh, we need You now to come and bind our wounds, to come and soothe our battle-weary souls. We need to know that You see us—that none of our tears have escaped Your notice and that it matters to You, this violence that has been done to our souls. Victorious Trinity, the One who is our Ezer, even as we are ezers, we call You into the battle and ask that You come into all the places where our lives are opposed, all the places where our enemy's jealousy and hatred has had a say. We bind oppression and mistreatment in Your name, Jesus. And we release on earth Your blessing over Your daughters, made in Your glorious image.*

Chapter 5

Twisted Eve

❦

> I think it is easy for me to focus on my wounded heart as bad and hurry to the healing, but Trinity is attracted to the beautiful mess—Can I view my own heart as a garden vs. something ugly, broken, unwanted and of no value until perfect? That is my invitation right now.
>
> —Ashley Thompson

In *The Lord of the Rings* trilogy, there is a character we are first introduced to as Gollum. Gollum is a very lonely and conflicted creature—at times helpful and drawn to the hope of friendship with Frodo while at other times entirely self-serving and manipulative, prone to betrayal and greed. He is also a rather unattractive sort, misshapen and rumpled, grotesque and frightening.

What we eventually learn is that before Gollum was Gollum, he was a hobbit named Sméagol who lived in a hobbit community and who had a family. Sméagol had teeth instead of Gollum's sharpened fangs. He wasn't stooped or misshapen or grotesque, and more importantly, Sméagol wasn't bound to betrayal and murder and greed. He only became those things, only became Gollum, when he was ensnared by the ring and made it his idol.

This is a tale literally as old as time. It is the story of humanity—our fall from glory and descent into ruin. It is the tale of Eve—an ezer who betrayed her charge, manipulated her mate, and exchanged her brilliant beauty for a more tarnished thing. And it is my story, and yours, dear daughter. Designed in the likeness of El Shaddai and Ruach HaKodesh, we too have chosen at points to follow in Eve's steps, and it led to our ruin, to our being twisted out of shape. This would be our final state and would have sealed a fate like Gollum's, except God. But I get ahead of myself.

In the once upon a time of Eve's story, we find the pattern for our own individual ruining. Until we see that for what it is we will continue to live as Twisted Eve, as Gollum, rather than from what was meant to be. For most of us, this twisted view of women and of ourselves is the easier one to believe. It is the version of the feminine which has lived the longest on the earth. And in our individual lives, it is the version of us that walks the planet up until the point that we meet redemption. Even then, the shedding of Twisted Eve is a gradual thing that reflects the process of *working out our salvation* and going from *glory to ever-increasing glory.* This process of healing, restoration, and sanctification is less about shaping up behavior (though that is a natural by-product) and more about getting to know the Trinity in a heart sort of way rather than just with our heads. This means experiencing Their goodness and Their goodness *for us*, becoming convinced of Their love and affection, and being settled that we belong in Their family. That's when gratitude really takes hold and transformation occurs in our understanding of who we are.

Before that happens, and in the earlier stages of our life with God, we live in a way that is more defined by the fall of Eden. I want to be specific about what this looked like for Eve and how it might come to us. It begins with what amounts to a Bible quiz: "Did God really say …?" Now, I can imagine that there is an innocent version of that question spoken by a heart that is searching to know God. But this isn't that. Since we have the advantage of knowing what comes next, imagine hearing this question through the tone of indignant outrage. Think of one teenager saying to another, in that tone that only teenagers can have, "Did your mom really tell you that you can't go to the party? You know everyone will be there." Or perhaps it was delivered in the slithery temptation tones of the classic bad boy, "Hello, gorgeous, I've got something you want, so forget what what's-his-name told you and come get it."

Whatever the approach, the serpent's conversation with Eve was meant to confuse her mind and stir the desires of her heart. This would throw her off balance enough that she would have trouble with the serpent's next quiz question. This is the test of whether Eve *knows the truth from a lie.* And this question is THE ONE that humanity has struggled with ever after,

Is God good?

Bound up in this question is another doozy,

Can you trust Him?

Much of my coaching work is with people who are recovering from emotional abuse. So let me tell you here and now that this is the moment when emotional abuse entered the world. These are hallmark tactics. Someone comes in a credible guise, in a position of knowledge or authority, or from a position of relationship, and they engage in lying, accusation, gaslighting, and sowing confusion. It is remarkably effective, dizzying even.

Eve's first moment of twisting came in her willingness to believe the worst about God, to entertain the accusation of God's enemy. This is still Satan's primary tactic, and we tend to experience it in our most vulnerable moments. Someone you love has been diagnosed with ovarian cancer which threatens her life and her chance of ever bearing children, a job has been pulled out from under you, a friendship has soured, or a marriage ended. It is in those moments of pain and feeling overwhelmed that we hear the whispers that "God is not good" or at least not for us. A thought passes through our minds, *You're all alone.* In the middle of a failure or bad choice you hear, "God hates you," or "God is disappointed in you." In the anxiety of the unknown when you really want help or comfort, there is the voice that says, "This is too little to bother God with," or worse, "This is petty. God doesn't care and thinks I am ridiculous, immature, selfish." And maybe hardest of all—in the dark of night, which is when everything seems worse—something in us cries out that *God has abandoned us,* and our hearts shrink in despair.

The accusations against God are endless. They often mimic experiences from our lives, especially the experiences we had in the families that raised us. I had a father who, though kind and loving, was a man of few words. So when I encountered silence from God and wondered, *Why won't God answer,* it felt familiar. I thought, *That's who God was as a parent.* The experiences may also have come from twisted church culture or at the hands of those who professed Christianity, "God is angry and just waiting to catch you in something so that punishment can be meted out."

While the accusations can show up as these statements about God, more often for us, they show up as anxiety. I know that firsthand as I lived much of my adolescence and early adulthood in an anxious place. I don't think people knew that about me since I disguised it pretty well in achievements and surface-level self-confidence. I was "mature" and responsible—a fairly typical firstborn. But underneath, I was just plain scared. The unknown was a really tough one, especially if I was expected to figure it out on the fly. I shied away from trying new things if I didn't think I'd immediately be good at them. And I expected so very much from myself. I didn't realize in those early years of my life that much of my anxiety was a form of not trusting God.

Years later, when I turned forty, Father did a very kind thing for me. It didn't feel kind in the beginning. In fact, it felt more like pure torture. But it saved my life, and I am grateful in a way that goes far beyond words. At that time, I was in my tenth year of being a professor and also had my own private practice as a psychologist. It had been a glorious few years, during which I felt very alive, but those years had also involved substantial cost and pouring out on my part. There was a deep exhaustion in my soul that I'd not yet admitted. When I heard the Holy Spirit ask me to quit my job and my practice, something in me leapt to immediate agreement. Of course, I assumed (yep, that word ... sigh ...) that Father was asking me to quit because He had a better opportunity for me, a job that would better fit the new longing that was forming in my heart. As it turned out, it *was* a better opportunity—to sit still and do nothing. *You've got to be kidding me!* I was good at a lot of things, but sitting still was definitely *not* one of them.

I felt like a caged animal, pacing one way and then another. I was angry and felt duped. God had tricked me into nothingness. Images came to mind of being a wolf caught in a trap, and I thought that if I could chew my foot off to get away, I just might consider that. And no, I'm not being dramatic. It felt that painful to me—I, who had been the poster child for multitasking and perpetual motion—but I couldn't bring myself to stage a jailbreak because this was God doing the asking. How do you refuse the God of the universe? And so I sat. Sort of. Still-ish. I was full of frustration and anger and pleading while hearing nothing. That echoed again my familiar experience of silence from a father. And like a mother with a small child who was fighting sleep, God let me struggle until I was tired of the effort and finally fell still in His presence.

Then it happened, that holy hush. Every morning, Father invited me to sit with Him on my back deck under the pergola covered in kiwi vines. We drank coffee, and I strummed my guitar, singing worship songs that repeated on a loop through my soul—the same sentence over and over and over; the words wouldn't let me go until the Spirit of God inhabited those words, inhabited the pergola and the space inside my soul. My Bible sat open, and I would feel drawn to a passage. Typically, I'd only get a sentence or so in and those words would capture me, and I'd hear the Trinity begin to talk about who They were, how They thought, and what They felt. Words! I was actually hearing words from God. The Trinity wasn't silent! And it was sweet, warm, and soothing to my heart. Something in me started to unwind.

It took another six months or so for me to realize what was happening, what God was after. This was about trust. This was about God's determination for me to know the Trinity more intimately, more experientially than I'd known was possible. You see, trust is the fruit of intimacy, the fruit of being transparent with another and finding that they are trustworthy. This was a season of learning that God would show up when my back was against the wall, when I needed things—practical and logistical things but also heart things. It was a process of finding out and coming to truly *believe* the answer to *why* God loved me. It turned out that it had nothing to do with my doing and everything to do with my being and existence. I couldn't fail my way out of God's heart or affection or presence any more than I could earn those things.

This became like a moment from the pages of my childhood when my family was on vacation in Tennessee, and my parents had the bright idea for the family to cross a long suspension bridge that was strung across a deep valley. My mother put me in front of her and began to encourage me to walk forward. *Uh-uh, no way.* I dug in my little heels with all my might and held onto the railing. I was *not* going across that crazy swaying thing and resisted the whole way. All the way until the midpoint when it occurred to me that there was less distance forward than backward, and I took off as fast as my little legs would go to get to the other side. The time with God became like that. The thing that I resisted and railed against became the thing my heart ran toward. Then I gladly sat still, grateful for Father's company, hanging on every word, trusting the Trinity in all the hard of those years. And yes, it was years. God spent a decade of my life sitting under a pergola.

I know that sounds crazy. It seemed like a strange use of my life, a wasteful use of time (how's that for an accusation!). And it was exactly what it would take for me to understand that the Trinity marches to a different drummer than I do. They value relationships over everything. They made us for union and intimacy. That is more important to Them than anything else I could have done with that time.

The Trinity knew what I didn't—that my heart had to become settled on the matter of Their goodness because everything else that followed in my life would depend on that. This was God addressing Twisted Eve in me, and it changed everything. This thing about the goodness of God is a lesson that has to be learned more than once because we need to see that it applies to every aspect of our lives. The decade of my sitting involved enduring situations that made me anxious—where would financial provision come from? How has my identity and sense of worth gotten wrapped around the job I do, the titles I wear, and the relationships I have? What do I have to show for myself at the end of a day with no clear accomplishments as I would normally define them? Did I hear God correctly about this sitting thing? It was a question that intensified as time wore on or as people in my life became uncomfortable with this choice.

God very systematically uncovered my anxieties and the lack of trust that lay behind them. It wasn't a very pretty picture, and I occasionally struggled with shame as I knew that trust was the right thing to do, but it wasn't the honest truth yet of where my heart was. And then there's the having to admit that to God. *Lord, I believe. Please heal my unbelief.* All of that forced me to grapple with how God felt about me in the moments of my incompleteness and half-heartedness. Down came any façade of perfection.

Where are the places of your mistrust? What are the moments in your life that your enemy has used opportunistically to create doubt and to sow lies about the goodness of God for you? What are the issues that anxiety uses to stalk you? What or who are the people in your life that you feel responsible for; have you been able to give that responsibility to Jesus? This tends to be a big thing for women—feeling responsible for the well-being and even for the happiness of people in our orbit. We tend to take on things that are not ours to bear. Finally, what are your questions about God, your questions to God?

After those years under the pergola, I am convinced that God is good. That is the anthem of my heart. No matter how it looks, no matter the outcome, no matter the cost, no matter what—I know that God is good, and I'm done with entertaining the lie that the Trinity isn't.

> *Dear Trinity, Abba Father, Amma Mother, Spirit of God, glorious Jesus—my continuous prayer is to know You, really know You. In all the spaces of my life, in all my needs and all my desires, and in all of Your glory and all of Your story, I want union with You—true intimacy—to see Your face and rest my head against Your heartbeat. I want to taste and see that You are good. Whatever it takes for that to be true, I'm in.*

The Second Source of Twisting

While Eve's troubles began with the serpent's initial gambit of *Did God really say,* they didn't end there. Having stirred up her desire, the serpent continues that goal by saying, "For God knows that on the day you eat from it your eyes will be opened [that is, you will have greater awareness], and you will be like God, knowing [the difference between] good and evil" (Genesis 3:5 AMP). This is an interesting ploy. It suggests that there is something good and desirable that the Trinity is keeping from Eve because God is greedy, wanting to withhold glory or position all to Themselves. This is a test of two things: Do you know in your deep places what God said about who you are, and do you believe that God is good?

You see, God had already declared that humankind was made in the likeness of the Trinity. Adam and Eve (and every other human) were already *like God.* This same strategy is played out in the desert where Jesus had fasted for forty days and then was confronted by Satan in three tests of His sonship. These also tested whether Jesus knew who He was in His sonship and in relation to Father. Both in this Eden moment, as well as in the desert, Satan offers something that is already ours to have while pretending that God would withhold it from us. The truth is that being *like God* is withheld from Satan; it was never part of his design. The angels were never meant to be like God, only to reflect some of the glory of God. Sonship and daughterhood are reserved for humanity and available to us at the moment that we come into adoption by the Trinity.

Being made *like God, in the image of God* is a glorious thing, but it's far different than *being God.* Humanity struggles with both halves of that truth. We greatly underestimate the meaningfulness of being made in God's image. It speaks to our nature and also our destiny. God told Adam he needed one like himself because Adam was not made to exist alone, and you can't have a deeply intimate relationship with something that is wholly unlike you. Mind you, it doesn't stop us from trying. That's what is so captivating about addictions. We develop a relationship with the thing we crave whether that is alcohol, exercise, pornography, or shopping. We have affection for that thing; spend time, money, and energy on it; and protect our time with it. Addictions function as affairs because they ensnare our hearts. But they are poor substitutes for other people and for God.

Because in love, the Trinity wanted children; because they wanted a bride for Jesus, They created us *like Themselves*. This was a purposeful move. They could have endowed any other of the creatures with the same likeness, but They didn't. Oh, They still love the critters, the land, the sky, the sea, but not like They love us. You, daughter, were made for relationship with the Trinity. It is fundamental to your design, and your life will not function well without it. There are parts of you—deep heart, mind, and soul parts—that can only be kept company by the living God. There are experiences of joy and beauty, adventure, and exhilaration that can only be had in the presence of God. And there is a reflected honor and delegated authority attached to being made like God that causes every other thing to give way to us—every angel, every demon, every created thing no matter how grand.

You are heir to the Kingdom of God and will reign as a queen alongside Jesus forever and ever. You are Cinderella incarnate. And the ruling and reigning isn't just about ball gowns and tiaras (though I do sometimes love the sparkly stuff). It's about power and authority and creativity and nurture. You will be called upon to rule and care for the world alongside your King and Lover.

Do you understand *who you are*? Are you preparing for that role? We aren't ready yet. We have to be healed into it, grow into it, and practice living it. And we have to lean into developing a love for our Husband that will allow us to live in union with Him and the rest of the Godhead. This includes living well with the truth that while we are like God, we aren't God. Patterned after El Shaddai and Ruach HaKodesh, yes. But Theirs is a glory that far exceeds ours. The Trinity will always know better than we do. To Them and Them alone belongs the right to define things like Truth, Love, Righteousness, and Goodness. Our place is to live in acknowledgment of that.

The testing of whether God is good comes through the

serpent redefining what is good. Satan tells Eve that the *knowledge* of good and evil is a desirable thing. On the surface, that seems reasonable. After all, isn't it a matter of wisdom to know the difference between the two? But here is the problem. The word used here for *knowledge* is a word that means experiential knowledge, not academic knowledge. In other words, knowing by being *engaged in* either as a recipient or as an initiator. Would it really be good for Eve to be the recipient of evil or to walk in evil herself? Is that kind of knowledge good? The Trinity knew that it wasn't. They had already experienced the evil of Lucifer's betrayal and knew firsthand the pain of that. It was the kindness of God to want to spare us from that sort of knowledge. Unfortunately, we tend not to be content with learning from others' experiences. We'd rather learn it the hard way. And oh, baby, did Eve learn it the hard way! This is played out over and over in humanity in general and our own stories in particular.

In Eve's agreement with the lie that there is something out there other than God that is worth her everything, she begins a journey into idolatry. We continue to make idols of things today, maybe not so much the knowledge of good and evil per se but often in the form of security, love, men, marriage, children, and jobs. These are obviously not bad things to long for in and of themselves. The problem is that sometimes we pursue *things* rather than or in greater priority than pursuing *God*. They become idols, and we become driven toward them by grasping and desperation at the expense of our own hearts and our relationship with God.

Eve made into an idol something that wasn't worth having. Again, there is an echo of this in Satan's test of Jesus in the desert. He promises Jesus the kingdoms of the world if Jesus will just do things Satan's way. Satan was offering Jesus a shortcut to what had already been declared, "The kingdom of the world has become the kingdom of our Lord and of his Messiah, and he will rule as king forever and ever" (Revelation

11:5 NOG). The problem with the shortcut was that the kingdoms of the world were, at that time, a ruined thing and not worth having. Their value fell far short of what Jesus would inherit at the end of the age when all was made new again.

The lesson here is twofold: Be careful what we call good, and be clear about its source. The answer to this test is found in truths like these,

> Every good thing given and every perfect gift is from above, coming down from the Father of lights, with whom there is no variation or shifting shadow. (James 1:17 NASB)

> For the LORD God is a sun and shield; The LORD bestows grace and favor and honor; *No good thing* will He withhold from those who walk uprightly. (Psalm 84:11 AMP, italics mine)

If our hearts aren't convinced of those truths, we will continue to make idols of things. And we will pursue those idols, driven by grasping and desperation, at the expense of our own hearts and of our relationship with God. We pursue the things God would willingly have given us in purer form, rather than pursuing God.

The Holy Spirit is still, in Her kindness, working to show me the idols I have embraced. Some of these are things that seem good and right but aren't as was true in the garden with Eve. More are things that are truly good but which have guidelines around them to keep them that way. For example, being loved in a romantic context is good unless we make choices to include inappropriate uses of our sexuality. Marriage is a good thing, ordained by the Trinity as a pattern and symbol of Their own union. Yet marriage isn't good between a redeemed heart that is turned toward God and a lost-in-sin-and-unbelief heart that is turned toward self as god. It prevents true union. A marriage

She

that includes the Trinity as a third strand in the chord is a good and right thing, but a marriage that isn't yoked to the culture of heaven is vulnerable to dynamics of abusiveness and the effects of selfishness. Accomplishment and doing things with excellence have a rightful place but not if we define our worth by them.

There are boundaries the Trinity draws around choices and experiences *for our own good*, in much the same way that parents set limits for their children and local governments set rules for driving. These are not born out of some wicked desire to control us for control's sake but rather to keep us safe and to create a culture that will support the fullness of life and the experience of love and delight and beauty and adventure.

But oh, my flesh seems to want what it wants when it wants it. The *when* part is really hard for me. While I am very patient with people, the same does not apply to my view of time. I'm a *right-now* kind of woman. And I struggle with this in things of God as well. When the Trinity lets me in on some intention They have toward my life or They reveal some new aspect of what I'm made for, my internal response is to say, "Let's get going then." It took me years to find my soul's pause button and even longer to want to use it. One of the truths of the Trinity that has dearly grated against my twisted self is that They value *process* as much or more than they value getting to the end destination.

For us to recover from this second kind of twisting means being able and willing to make a stand on the goodness of God, trusting that goodness to be active in every moment of our lives. As my friends at Zoweh ask, "What is the good God is up to in your life?" It helps to know the answer to that, and if you don't, ask the Trinity to show you. We must cultivate a heart that expects goodness and grace to be around every corner, present in every situation, pursuing us with every breath. If we can trust the Trinity not just to be good but to be good *for us*, then we are much less likely to make idols of things that don't deserve our attention and pursuit.

The Results of Twisting

In choosing to act outside of God's instructions, Twisted Eve immediately experienced a series of consequences, many of which are connected to relationships. The most serious of them came from her inherent rejection of the Trinity's fathering and mothering of her. She stepped outside of that covering and relationship even as the prodigal son did in that powerful parable. In that moment, Eve became orphaned and subject to the orphan spirit. This is the same spirit that characterized her enemy. Lucifer once had a place in heaven. He belonged there, was welcome there, and was protected and provided for by the Most High God. But Lucifer's rebellion cost him his home and all of the provision and glory he had once enjoyed. Fallen from the house of God, he lost his beauty and his position as a trusted angel. Now he had to beg, borrow, and steal his way through life with no one to look out for him.

This is the kingdom that Twisted Eve chose, so she became orphaned too, lost from the face of the Trinity, and separated from Their love, provision, and protection. It isn't that the Trinity no longer loved her or wanted her but that she separated herself from that love when she left the home she had through relationship with Them. Eve also lost the inheritance that had been hers of authority over the earth and ruling and reigning with Jesus.

It is impossible to overstate the impact of the orphan spirit. It is the source of most anxiety, fear, and striving. Orphan-ness is what produces our sense of abandonment and of feeling small in the world. It is a state devoid of comfort or nurture. And it speaks to our hearts that we are unlovable and unwanted.

The largest problem with an orphan identity is that it cannot be healed by the usual things we throw at problems. Achievement won't do it, nor will education, service, self-protection, a social media following, or general busyness. An orphan heart is only healed when it returns to Father and Mother. It is only healed in relationship with the Trinity. Theirs is the only parenting that provides a True mirror of who we are. Their heart is the only one that sings a consistent song of love and adoration over our lives.

Dear one, until you come home to Abba and to Amma (El Shaddai)—until you are held close against Their heartbeat and look into Their faces, this wound will continue to chase you. You are Someone's much-loved daughter. You've been wanted all the days of your life. You belong at the family table, at the place set just for you. You don't have to worry whether there's room for you, and you can be sure that if you go missing from your place, all of heaven will notice and go looking for you. You matter to God. Your birth was not an accident or a surprise (no matter the earthly circumstances surrounding your arrival here). Ultimately, you are not just a person, a human being, or a woman. You are a *daughter, a much-loved daughter.* Take that into your soul, and speak it over your own life regardless of how you might feel at any given moment. Allow the Spirit of God to breathe on it, and you will find that it puts an end to the orphan identity that happened in your twisting.

Left unhealed, our twisting and orphan identity invades our relationships with people too; the damage is not contained just to our life with God. It causes us to misperceive other's intentions and to live in some level of mistrust toward them. We act out of a self-protective mode, and that always has the effect of compromising our ability to love others well. We can see this pattern in Eve's life as she turns from being a daughter to being an orphan and then betrays her life with Adam. Adam also becomes twisted in his own orphan-ness, laying down his life as a son and betraying the wife who was bone of his bone and flesh of his flesh. It has been like that ever after in each generation of their sons and daughters down to this very day.

We've talked already about Eve's betrayal of her *role* of ezer kenegdo in Adam's life. Neither of them recognized that the conversation with the serpent was an act of war. Neither raised a sword against the serpent nor in defense of one another (the function of an ezer kenegdo). But Eve didn't just fail as an ezer; she also betrayed her *relationship* with Adam even as he betrayed his relationship with Eve.

Stand in that moment with me. There is a series of dynamics set in motion here. As the serpent strikes up a conversation with Eve, she faces her enemy alone. Even though Adam is physically present with her, he is silent and fails to act—the beginning of Adam's twisting and his betrayal of Eve. This creates a wound in Eve that says she is alone and cannot count on Adam. So begins her fear of abandonment and her quest to never experience it again. Being left to fend for herself, Eve agrees with the accusation against God and accepts the invitation to take her life into her own hands. She begins to grasp for what the serpent has told her is good and encourages Adam to do the same.

Eve is Adam's wife, his intimate partner in life, and his closest companion. Father has already spoken into Adam's heart-need for her. Father has also said that to eat the fruit of this particular tree will mean Adam's death. Do you see the impossible position he's in? Eve has already fallen, temporarily blinded by a lie. Now she uses her relationship capital. When she offers to share the fruit with Adam, this moment isn't simply about whether he too believes the lie. It is also about whether he wants to risk losing her if God has, in fact, told the truth. If Adam doesn't also eat the fruit, he will have to do life without her. He will be alone again as he was before her creation. Adam chooses Eve over God, beginning his own journey into idolatry.

In the moments following their disastrous choices, we gain a glimpse of how Adam's view of Eve begins to shift. Her betrayal of him created a wound in Adam that speaks to his heart that he cannot trust Eve. She will use her beauty and relationship capital for his ruin. As a result, he now lives suspiciously of Eve, which likely means living with a guarded, self-protected heart. He is drawn to her beauty and knows at some level that

She

she is meant to be part of him yet is simultaneously repelled by mistrust. Adam develops the new belief that Eve is not a good thing. We see this displayed when confronted by God, Adam blames both God and Eve, referring to her as "the woman You gave me." The insinuation here is that God gave Adam a bad gift, that Eve herself *is* a bad gift. The blame-shifting is part of a larger pattern of Adam's failure to take responsibility.

Another unfortunate relationship dynamic of Eve's twisting comes from the penalty God imposes on her because Eve has harmed Adam. Her previously equal partnership with Adam will change to him *ruling over her*. This is not humanity's original design or the Trinity's desire for their relationship, but rather a result of Eve's choice. Also important to see is that the *ruling over* as God speaks it in Genesis 3 does not have the connotation of harm or slavery but comes from a word suggesting differential power or authority. However, as many of our stories will bear witness, over the generations this new organizational chart became the source of terrible abuse of women at the hands of men including verbal, emotional, physical, and spiritual mistreatment. Again I want to be clear that this is not the Trinity's intention in the consequence They handed out, but rather the ripple effect of Adam's mistrust and devaluing of Eve, along with his shame of showing up so poorly for her. The ripples intensify with each generation.

The only good news in this is that redemption produces its fruit in us even now, making us able to right these relationship issues in a progressive way *in this present life*. The even better news is that as the Trinity makes all things new and redemption has its full effect at the end of the age, these dynamics will change back to what God intended all along.

> The Spirit of the Lord GOD is upon me, because the LORD has anointed me to bring good news to the poor; he has sent me to bind up the brokenhearted, to proclaim liberty to the captives,

> and the opening of the prison to those who are bound ... to give them a beautiful headdress instead of ashes, the oil of gladness instead of mourning, the garment of praise instead of a faint spirit; that they may be called oaks of righteousness, the planting of the LORD, that he may be glorified. *They shall build up the ancient ruins; they shall raise up the former devastations; they shall repair the ruined cities, the devastations of many generations.* (Isaiah 61:1, 3–4 ESV, emphasis mine)

The Faces of Self-Protection

Fueled by anxiety, shame, abandonment, and unmet need, Eve covered herself with both literal and emotional fig leaves of self-protection in her life with Adam. This is handed down through the generations. These self-protective fig leaves of ours are different than the concept of guarding our hearts as seen in Proverbs 4:23. The latter comes from a place of wisdom and is aimed at protecting the heart from damage and corruption so that we remain alive and well. This allows us to reflect our highest glory and to walk in the integrity of the Trinity. In contrast, the fig leaves version comes from a place of anxiety and shame and is aimed at keeping our brokenness from view by hiding our twisted state. This produces a false self that is far less beautiful and healthy than our authentic self.

If you can't count on Adam to come through as Eve learned in the encounter with the serpent, then life feels lonely and chaotic. Perhaps you have found this to be true in life with your Adam as well or before that in life with your father or other significant male figures. Chaos causes us not to know what to count on. In response and in reaction, we use control to steady ourselves, to create the illusion that chaos can be tamed, and to make ourselves feel safe and provided for. Deep desperation

She

fuels all of that, as well as the fear that our efforts may fail. When we grow exhausted by pursuit and by the nagging sense that nothing is going to truly satisfy our starving hearts, we abandon the chase and resign ourselves to whatever crumbs we can find of regard, provision, or safety.

In the hands of our false selves, our self-protective strategies become means for securing the things that our desperate desire sets its sights on. The first version of this involves demanding that life, circumstances, and people operate as we want. In practical terms, control feels rigid both to us and others, though we generally clothe it in a more favorable spin. Perhaps we pass it off as just wanting to be able to plan ahead or prepare, and we get bent out of shape when things don't go our way or as expected. We might call it being responsible, mature, or knowing what we want. Often there is a bit of perfectionism thrown in that we might apply to ourselves and others. In the end, the drive for control causes our insides to feel tightly wound, and our physical bodies may display the stress of that in illness, fatigue, ulcers, or poor sleep. You might find it hard to relax, and breathing deeply takes effort. Slowing down is hard. This was my state before Father called that long time-out in my life in order to heal my trust issues.

The other common version of self-protection involves figuring out how to twist ourselves into whatever others want so that they will be pleased with us. If we can please them, then maybe they will offer us relationships, protection, provision, favor, status, opportunity, or pleasure. This twisting might manifest as withholding our voices and *going along to get along*. This inevitably leads to emotional dishonesty on our part. It could look like accepting false responsibility for the feelings of others or for the outcomes of their choices. Whatever form it takes when we become a reflection of what another wants, we give up our true selves and may allow others to treat us poorly, even abusively. We settle for whatever we can get rather than risk losing it all. I wish that I had better understood that earlier in my life. It would have saved me years of hurt that came from living in a marriage characterized by emotional abuse, neglect, and my spouse's addictions—the things he loved more than me.

Daughter, I want to encourage you to be brave—brave enough to look at your false self and all of its strategies and ways of being. Brave enough to bring it before God and exchange it for truth, vulnerability, and healing. Courage will be needed because this means laying aside the things we have long trusted—our orphan ways of looking out for ourselves—and instead asking for God's help and trusting the Trinity's goodness for you. But I promise that if you will engage in that journey, it will lead to freedom and more spacious places for your soul.

> He brought me out into a spacious place;
> he rescued me because he delighted in me.
> —Psalm 18:19 NIV

Holy Trinity, I remind my soul of Your great love for me and Your commitment to bring me to a place of wholeness. I'm grateful that You embrace me in my woundedness so that you can heal me. You welcome me into Your presence even in my sin so that You can wash me clean of it. I know that my heart is safe with You and so I ask that You "search me [thoroughly], O God, and know my heart; Test me and know my anxious thoughts; And see if there is any wicked or hurtful way in me, And lead me in the everlasting way." (Psalm 139:23–24 AMP)

Chapter 6

To Mother, a Verb

A significant part of recovering from our twisted state comes from living in greater awareness of how we are made—with a beauty all our own and a design that is glorious because it reflects the glory of the One. You are an image of the Trinity in all Their brilliant splendor. You are cut from that cloth, and your DNA contains courage, strength, compassion, and intimacy. God made you that way because it pleases Them, because the Trinity finds you beautiful. And just as we marvel at the faces of our children, your existence brings joy to God.

Within that circle of relationship between you and God, there is peace, rest, and union. God enjoys collaborative dreaming with you and invites you to partner in acts of life and creativity. If that's all the purpose and meaning that your existence served, it is more than enough. *You* are *more than enough.*

Yet incredibly, you, daughter, were made for even more. God chose to create a world that needs you and depends on you to be who you are designed to be. And without that, creation is a lesser place. I'm not trying to fluff you up. This is not a cheerleading moment (trust me, I've been a cheerleader and it isn't my best thing). Nor is this kindness or optimism run amok. It is simply truth, taken from scripture, from the story God is telling. I'll borrow a line from Sgt. Joe Friday, "All [I] know are the facts, ma'am."

The *even more* of our lives is connected to another of our views of the *she-ness* of God—the Holy Spirit, Ruach HaKodesh. Much of the Spirit's activity in the world exemplifies the verb, to mother. Remember that our first introduction to the Spirit of God shows Her brooding over the waters of creation like a mother hen with her chicks. We're going to use the ministry and nature of the Holy Spirit to better understand our own design. This, dear one, is what is meant to flow from your life.

Nurturing as Provision

Mother is not just a noun but also a verb. To *mother* involves acts of nurturing, *the care, encouragement, and development of a whole person—their body, mind, and spirit.* Nurture is related to the verb *cultivate* which means *to protect and encourage the growth of, to cause to grow by special attention, and to improve by labor and care.* Because human beings are made of many parts all housed in the same being, nurturing needs to be offered toward all of those parts—body, soul, mind, and spirit—lest the whole person suffer. Physically feeding someone goes beyond just the care of their body. It also translates into communicating care for the other parts of them. You cannot separate our parts; that is not how we function.

As an example of that, I led a Bible study for a time which met at my house on Friday nights. Several of the women had to rush straight from work and didn't have time for dinner, so over time, it seemed a natural thing for me to offer dinner before the Bible study. For myself, I found delight in preparing food for others and considering them as I planned the menu. What would bring them joy? How could I make the meal both delicious and beautiful? It was an offering of consideration of them and of my creative heart and willing hands. It is oddly satisfying to feed others, meeting a need in my own soul as much as it meets the needs of their bodies.

There is something holy that happens when you set a table for people to gather 'round over food and conversation. This simultaneous nurturing of body and soul is healing, restorative, and restful—a thing of joy and belonging, of welcome and companionship. To be invited there, to be invited close to others, and to receive what they've prepared and poured out with you in mind—this is its own form of intimacy and community.

Our time around the table was warm and comforting. We saw and were seen. Together we created a place where hearts joined together even if only briefly, and we felt less alone and more connected. We lingered longer, and in the lingering found that dinner and Bible study became one thing, one seamless experience of one another and of God.

Whenever I hear the word *table,* I think of Psalm 23:5 which is typically rendered something like *you set a table before me in the presence of my enemies. You anoint my head with oil; my cup overflows.* And if that was the only version of it, this picture would be enough—the Trinity coming even when we're under siege to make provision for us, food for our bodies, a place of respite and refreshing for our souls. This feels like nurture within the context of the real world, especially in the space of adulting where life can be hard and trying.

For so many women, our daily experience is of having to set a table for ourselves. What would it be like for you to hear the invitation of God to come to a table already set for you by Someone who loves you? An invitation to come rest away from the fray of life; to be fed and nurtured, to share the company of the Trinity in sweet companionship? As I contemplate this invitation, my soul is flooded with scriptures where God promises provision. There are passages like the lilies of the field clothed in splendor and the birds who don't sow or reap, yet God provides for them. Then comes the Trinity's grand point—that you are loved far more than the birds and flowers and *will be cared for* out of the storehouse of God's heart and kingdom. I'm reminded of God's immense kindness to convince my heart that those promises can be trusted.

There is another translation of Psalm 23 which adds a whole new layer to it. In The Passion Translation, verse 5 reads,

> You become my delicious feast even when my enemies dare to fight. You anoint me with the fragrance of your Holy Spirit; you give me all I can drink of you until my cup overflows.

This is the abundance of nurturing present in El Shaddai—Mother God whose milk never runs out and who always has enough for us and always is enough for us. This is the voice I heard one day when I was crying out for God to heal someone I loved who lay gravely ill. The voice that replied that not only could I have all of God's stuff, but I could have all of God, all that the Trinity is in Their essence—love, compassion, wisdom, power, and strength. God was willing to give me access to Their very being for me and for those who cross my path. Hear me, dear one. The Trinity wants to feed you, to nurture you, to pour into your being *who They are*. Their desire is to be so in union with you that it is as though you and They are one. And in that union, your life is so fully supplied, so fully met, and so fully held that it overflows onto those around you. Such overflow even reaches the critters and the earth itself. This is why Romans 8:19 (TPT) says that

> the entire universe is standing on tiptoe, yearning to see the unveiling of God's glorious sons and daughters! For against its will the universe itself has had to endure the empty futility resulting from the consequences of human sin. But now, with eager expectation, all creation longs for freedom from its slavery to decay and to experience

She

with us the wonderful freedom coming to God's children.

Hospitality is inherent in the concept of nurture. To nurture another requires that we invite them—into our physical space, into our hearts, and into our own vulnerability as we offer something of ourselves. It is also an invitation for others to receive from us, which is its own kind of vulnerability. I can't stress this enough. Both the offering and the receiving of nurture involve intimacy. You cannot engage it with your heart held back. Because of this, nurturing includes creating an environment of safety as a foundation for vulnerability. What does it mean then, in the human landscape, for Ruach HaKodesh to do this for us and how do we, in turn, do this for others?

Nurturing as Protection and Safety

> Listen to me, O house of Jacob, all the remnant of the house of Israel, who have been borne by me from your birth, carried from the womb, even to your old age I am he, even when you turn gray I will carry you. I have made, I will bear; I will carry and will save. (Isaiah 46:3–4 ESV)

While we tend to think of mothers in nurturing roles, there is a fierce side to a mother's heart. This is why the phrase "mama bear" needs little explanation. Our imaginations immediately hear the roar and see the teeth aimed at any intruder who intends to harm her little ones. Interestingly, scripture uses similar images to portray the mother heart of God though more often through the form of birds rather than bears. Here again, I'm reminded of our first view of Ruach HaKodesh, the hovering or brooding Spirit of God who moves over the water in Genesis like a mother hen brooding over her chicks. As another example, Jesus, in weeping compassion over Jerusalem, talks about his desire to protect and embrace them,

> "How often I have longed to gather your children together, as a hen gathers her chicks under her wings." (Luke 13:34 NIV)

Perhaps most famously, Psalm 91 uses similar themes.

> He who dwells in the shelter of Elyon, will abide in the shadow of Shaddai. I will say of ADONAI, "He is my refuge and my fortress, my God, in whom I trust. For He will rescue you from the hunter's trap and from the deadly pestilence. He will cover you with His feathers, and under His wings you will find refuge. His faithfulness is body armor and shield. You will not fear the terror by night, nor the arrow that flies by day, nor the plague that stalks in darkness, nor the scourge that lays waste at noon. A thousand may fall at your side, and ten thousand at your right hand, but it will not come near you. You will only look on with your eyes and see the wicked paid back. (Psalm 91:1–8 TLV)

Safety conjures up the image of being free from harm and danger. There is certainly a version of harm and danger that applies to our physical selves, and even here we see the Holy Spirit at work. I love the story my friend Bob tells of being a young man stationed in the army and posted to Germany. Bob was still very lost and adrift in life at that point. He spent his off time drinking, partying, and living oblivious to God and to his own soul.

One night, returning to base from a night of bar hopping, a very drunk and unsteady Bob stood on the edge of the curb

She

about to cross the street. It was late. No one else was in sight. Suddenly out of nowhere, Bob heard an urgent voice saying, "Stand still. Don't take another step!" The voice was so startling and compelling that Bob obeyed without even knowing why. About that time, a car came tearing down the street at high speed and passed right in front of Bob's nose. If he had taken a single step forward, his life would likely have ended then and there. Instead, there stood a shaken and quickly sobering Bob, who realized that he had just had an encounter with God. He would later come to know that this was the voice of Ruach HaKodesh, the Spirit of God. Thus began a stunningly beautiful new season of his life that continues to this day. Another one of my friends heard the Holy Spirit instruct him to begin a vegetarian lifestyle. In my own life, I was impressed by Ruach HaKodesh to do certain dietary things to bolster my immune system.

Since the Holy Spirit is, well, a *spirit*, we sometimes overlook Her desire to nurture all of us, our whole being. And while it's true that your soul's health has a greater impact on eternity, that doesn't mean the Trinity is unconcerned about your physical health. God wants to nurture every part of you. After all, the Spirit of God is a life-giving force (Romans 8:2, 5)—the very breath of life who animated Adam, turning him from a lifeless form into a living being (Genesis 2:7). It was the Spirit who raised Jesus's physical body from the dead (Romans 8:11). What might it look like for you to make space for the Holy Spirit to love on your physical body and to usher in the healing that Jesus purchased for you? What if you were open to God offering instruction about how to live well? What if you asked God to breathe fresh life into your worn and weary places?

> *Ruach HaKodesh, Spirit of the Living God, You are intimately acquainted with my body. You were there at its design and creation; Your breath brought me to life, and You have brooded over*

Lenne' Hunt

> *me all of my days. You know every cell of my being, every strand of my DNA. You have seen the physical load that stress has put on my body, the places that store trauma, grief, and pain. You are aware of any injury or disease commissioned against my life—to rob, kill, and destroy. I invite You in Ruach HaKodesh, Spirit of my Jesus, my Redeemer and Healer who purchased health for my body even as for my soul. Come and refresh my body. Restore it to the order of heaven and lead me in its care.*

Then beyond the physical, how does the Holy Spirit create safety for our hearts, minds, and souls? A significant aspect of safety comes from that secure attachment we discussed earlier. In secure bonding, the message is twofold: the worth of the one being loved and the heart of the one offering it. If the offer is conditional or unpredictable, safety isn't possible. Mothers don't hold babies at their breasts because the child accomplished something. They don't feed their children based on whether the child obeyed or met some milestone as expected. Deuteronomy 10:15 says that the Trinity loved Israel and *set Their affection* on them. This reflects a choice the Trinity made to invest Their hearts in Israel, to pour out Their hearts on the children of Their house on earth. This is the *all-in* moment of parenthood. "You are *mine*, my child, birthed from my heart. And you have all of my heart's affection and compassion, care and concern. My eyes are on you, and I will spend the resources and energy of my life to prosper yours." This is the well from which nurture flows in provision and protection for the beloved.

It is here again that we encounter the mother bear part of nurturing, that fierce thing that throws itself between us and all that stalks our lives. The Trinity is clear about how they regard injustice and mistreatment of all that They have made and faithfully love—sometimes so clear it is frightening. For example,

> You shall not mistreat any widow or fatherless child. If you do mistreat them, and they cry out to me, I will surely hear their cry, and my wrath will burn, and I will kill you with the sword, and your wives shall become widows and your children fatherless. (Exodus 22:22–24 ESV)

The Trinity goes to great lengths in scripture to give instruction as to how we are to treat one another. For example,

> "If you lend money to any of my people with you who is poor, you shall not be like a moneylender to him, and you shall not exact interest from him. If ever you take your neighbor's cloak in pledge, you shall return it to him before the sun goes down, for that is his only covering, and it is his cloak for his body; In what else shall he sleep? And if he cries to me, I will hear, for I am compassionate." (Exodus 22:25–27 ESV)

So many of the people I walk alongside have a history of mistreatment and abuse both in their families of origin and in their marriages. The pain and injury are profound, and so is their sense of injustice. I'll tell you what I tell them. Do not underestimate the fierceness of God's love for you. Unless your abusers repent before God in a way that is humble and true of heart and unless they find the forgiveness of Jesus over their lives, what they have perpetrated against you will lead to their death. God will not excuse or turn a blind eye to the ways in which you have been harmed. And the Trinity pledges that Their fierce love will rise up in protection. This too is nurture.

That is the degree to which the Trinity has set their affection on you.

> "Because of the violence done to the oppressed, because of the painful cries of the needy, I will spring into action,"[1] says the LORD. "I will provide the safety they so desperately desire." (Psalm 12:5 NET)

> Say to those who have an anxious heart, "Be strong; fear not! Behold, your God will come with vengeance, with the recompense of God. He will come and save you." (Isaiah 35:4 ESV)

> But the LORD is with me as a dread champion [one to be greatly feared]; Therefore my persecutors will stumble and not overcome [me]. They will be completely shamed, for they have not acted wisely and have failed [in their schemes]; Their eternal dishonor will never be forgotten. (Jeremiah 20:11 AMP)

Make no mistake. Your life's well-being matters to the Trinity, and They pledged to defend you and to make right any harm that comes to you. The mother heart of God will not rest until there is peace for you—a wholeness of body, soul, spirit, heart, mind, and will. Any good mother wants that for her children. We work for our children's good; we look for ways to nourish them, both their bodies and their spirits. We protect our children's vulnerabilities and tend to their scraped knees and bruised hearts. And we rise up in great ferocity to defend them, often putting ourselves in harm's way. The heart of a good mother is to spend herself on her children's welfare. And the heart of Mother God is no different. She offers refuge and protection.

El Shaddai, teach me to look to You as my refuge and forgive me when I run to places other than You. Seal the truth of Your fierce love in my heart so that I trust You with the whole of my welfare. Holy Spirit, let me sense You hovering over my life in love and watchfulness, offering compassion and a place of protection.

Nurturing as Wisdom, Mentoring, and Encouragement

Then a shoot will come out from the stump of Jesse, and a branch from its roots will bear fruit. The Ruach Yahweh will rest on him—the Ruach of wisdom and understanding, the Ruach of advice and power, the Ruach of knowledge and fear of Yahweh. (Isaiah 11:1–2 NOG)

Another way in which Ruach HaKodesh offers protection is found in Her role as the administrator of the spirit of wisdom (also represented in Hebrew as a *she*). Rabbi Rami Shapiro writes, "Chochma [Hebrew for wisdom] was not simply the first of God's creations; She was the means through which all the others came forth. Chochma is both created and creative. She is the ordering principle of creation. ... She illumines everything. She is right seeing ... She is the Way God is manifest in the world. To know Her is to know God as well."[10]

We live in an age where common sense is no longer common and wisdom has gone missing altogether, so the prospect of Ruach HaKodesh offering that to us is a pretty big deal. *Right seeing.* Wow, that alone is everything. In this generation, everything is about individual truth, blurred lines, and subjective definitions. We are confronted by complex

---

[10] . The Divine Feminine in Biblical Wisdom Literature: Selections Annotated & Explained, SkyLight Illuminations (2005) by Rabbi Rami Shapiro and Rev. Cynthia Bourgeault PhD

issues of social justice and don't get me started on the state of American politics. How are we to know the right perspective, the one that aligns with Truth? We are mentored by the Spirit of God who administrates the spirit of wisdom. From Her, we learn how to order our steps, how to see rightly, and how to walk in creativity to birth things on the earth. There is so much protection in the voice of Wisdom and so much love and nurturing in a God who offers that to us.

The Holy Spirit also leads us into life by reminding us and explaining to our hearts the things that Jesus said and did when He walked the earth. Much of our emotional and spiritual safety is tied to the boundaries the Holy Spirit sets for us. Those boundaries mark the territory in which we can live without harm, but outside of which, harm is sure to find us. I'm speaking here about the boundaries that define righteousness and which produce clean hands and hearts. If I walk in the paths of kindness and truth, forgiveness, compassion, heart integrity, and uprightness, I will be kept safe from guilt and shame. I will not injure my own heart or my relationships.

The kind of safety and protection we're talking about here is a mirror for the safety and protection that is given to babies who nurse at their mother's breasts. In addition to all of the other benefits of nursing, the baby also gains access to their mother's immune system. In feeding from the mother's essence, the baby's body inherits the protection she carries against infections. It is the same when we feed from Ruach HaKodesh, taking into our hearts, souls, minds, and beings Her wisdom and counsel. The life of the Spirit in us produces the fruit of peace, making us whole and without injury.

If I am honest, I have to admit that there are moments when I refuse to be nurtured. It's the behavior of a child who refuses to eat the food that's been prepared for her dinner or who gets tired, fussy, and uncooperative with what the parent has planned. Even more blatantly, sometimes in an all-out moment of emotional immaturity and just plain rebellion, I strike out on my own—crossing those well-meant boundary lines and behaving like I was raised by wolves rather than by the Spirit of God. But even in the moments where I pull a Twisted Eve and make my own way, Ruach HaKodesh leads me to repentance and restores me again to God and to myself. The Trinity's unconditional love rescues me from me and brings me back to warmth and safety again.

The Holy Spirit's mentoring of us occurs in the context and with the attitude of love. Ruach HaKodesh does not come as a drill sergeant commanding our obedience but rather with care, kindness, and affection. She appeals to the best in us, speaking Wisdom from Her deep places to ours. There is no judgment or accusation in Her mothering of us. She only has the desire for us to truly live, be well, and be at peace. I'm amazed at the Spirit's ability to call me up higher, to a better and more sanctified existence without it feeling religious or dry. She creates in me the desire to be who I'm meant to be in gratitude for all the Trinity has poured out for my life.

And the patience, oh, the patience! The attitude of the Holy Spirit reminds me of my father, a dear soul who is also long in the patience department. I got a really good view of my father's patience at the age of twelve when, inspired by Chrissie Evert (yes, I'm that old), I begged my father to teach me to play tennis. He graciously agreed, and armed with my brand-new flaming-orange Chris Evert tennis racquet, off we went to the courts. Day after painful day, my patient father fed me balls and instructions and watched me fail miserably. We spent far more time chasing errant balls than actually hitting them. It would take another decade for my coordination to catch up to my body, and my father persevered through all of that. Over the years, playing with him was such a thing of joy. His patient, kind coaching set the tone for me so that I never resisted the coaching of others who came alongside me in that tennis journey. He taught me not to fear instruction and not to lose heart in the process.

Jesus introduces us to Ruach HaKodesh as the "Helper (Comforter, Advocate, Intercessor—Counselor, Strengthener, Standby), the Holy Spirit, whom the Father will send in My name [in My place, to represent Me and act on My behalf], He will teach you all things. And He will help you remember everything that I have told you" (John 14:26 AMP). This is an echo of Psalm 32:8 (NIV), "I will instruct you and teach you in the way which you should go; I will counsel you with My loving eye upon you."

Instruction and mentoring are such an important part of nurture. What has been your experience of being mentored *as a woman, in your relationships, in your mothering, in the work of your hands, or in shepherding your own beauty?* These are not simple things. And there are many voices out there telling us who and how to be. But can those voices be trusted to represent Truth—do they speak from a heart of love for us and a desire to see us whole and flourishing? I think of Rear Admiral Grace Hopper whose accomplishments in life could easily fill a book yet revealed her truest heart by saying, "The most important thing I've accomplished, other than building the compiler, is training young people. I keep track of them as they get older and I stir 'em up at intervals so they don't forget to take chances."

If you're like most of us, you have questions that need asking. But some questions are hard to ask because they reveal our vulnerability, our undone-ness. We wonder if we're the only ones who don't know the answer. Or maybe the thought occurs that we're the only one who struggles with this or feels that way or has experienced that thing. Maybe we will meet judgment if we ask. It's heartbreaking to me that the voices of shame and accusation so often rise up to prevent us from asking. Where instead are the voices of compassion and wisdom that would rise up to gently receive us in all of the places where we are still becoming and as we are untwisting ourselves and pursuing whole life and truth?

> *Ruach HaKodesh, Spirit of God, Spirit of wisdom and counsel, we need You. Would You cause our hearts to know that You welcome our questions and our undone-ness? Let us sit in Your compassion and gentle, kind regard for us. Amma God, we ask in humility, willing to receive Your wisdom. We lay down our panic and the anxiety of all we do not know and enter the rest of the One who knows everything, the One who knows us. Help us to grow into the beauty You built into our design so that it colors our choices, our attitudes, our relationships, and our life's work. Lead us down the path of grace and mercy as we receive, and then offer, the nurturing that You bring to our lives.*

The journey of becoming is long, often strewn with rocks, beset by detours and delays, and more often uphill than is comfortable. I get frustrated with myself, especially in moments of backtracking and stumbling. In the midst of those moments, I've come to appreciate the encouragers in my life. My mom is really good at encouraging—and it isn't just that she stands on the sidelines and cheers. She also joins me in the pursuit of my dreams, helping to make them possible. Over the years, Mom has encouraged me from her vantage point of editor for my books and creative collaborator during my art studio years. She has been willing to dream with me and to fuel my excitement. How much harder it would have been without her.

My friend Hilary also has a strong gift of encouragement. As she walked with the Holy Spirit in that gift, she would often encounter resistance from those to whom she offered encouragement. They would brush her words aside or paint them as her being *sweet*, nice, etc. I remember her having to explain the difference between encouragement and all those other words. She would say that encouragement is rooted in Truth, in the very Kingdom of God. It wasn't a product of sweetness or people pleasing or just wanting folks to feel better. Instead, it came from her collaboration with the Spirit, hearing Ruach HaKodesh whisper the truth of a person in her ear so that Hilary could then call them up higher into that truth. She would offer the encouragement that *there was more* to themselves than what they've allowed or considered. And she would prod them to receive God's pronouncement over their lives that they were enough for this; they were tailor-made and handpicked by God for the things their hearts were drawn toward.

This is the ministry of the Spirit in our lives who doesn't stop at instruction and mentoring but goes further, pressing us to believe the truth of our own design. The Spirit calls us to own what God has entrusted to us—not walking in false humility which often takes the form of representing ourselves and what we have to offer as something small. True humility doesn't ask that we deny the truth of ourselves but that we don't see our gifts as originating within ourselves. This means becoming convinced in our hearts that the Author of all that is good, has also authored us, and given us goodness and glory to shepherd on behalf of the Kingdom for the sake of creation.

Nurturing as Comfort

> In all their distress He was distressed, and the angel of His presence saved them, In His love and in His compassion He redeemed them; And He lifted them up and carried them all the days of old. (Isaiah 63:9 AMP)

> Drink deeply of her glory even as an infant drinks at its mother's comforting breasts. "This is what the LORD says: "I will give Jerusalem a river of peace and prosperity. The wealth of the nations

will flow to her. Her children will be nursed at her breasts, carried in her arms, and held on her lap. I will comfort you there in Jerusalem as a mother comforts her child." (Isaiah 66:11–13 NLT)

Comfort is an essential expression of nurturing. It holds us in grief, speaks hope in the midst of despair, quiets our fear and anxiety, and tells us that all is well, and we will be OK. Comfort reminds us that the pain is not all there is and won't last forever. It speaks truth overtop the lies and accusations that have come against us. It leads us to courage and calls us to rise up again.

Comfort is central to El Shaddai and Ruach HaKodesh. This is the mother heart of God which draws us in tenderness to be held in her embrace. And so we return again to the hospitality and invitation of nurture. Mother God opens Herself—Her own heart and being. She opens Herself to us *because She has set Her affection on us, because we are Her beloved.* We are the ones She has borne in Her likeness. We are the daughters of El Shaddai, of Ruach HaKodesh, and because of that, our lives are imprinted on Her hands. There is never a moment, a breath we breathe, that is outside of Her seeing and knowing. Mother God opens Her heart and arms to us, and then She draws us with the invitation to embrace and be embraced. This is where comforting begins, in the seeing and knowing of another.

You might be familiar with another of God's names revealed in scripture: Yahweh Jireh (or you may have heard it as Jehovah Jireh) which we translate as *God who provides*. But the fuller meaning in the Hebrew is *God who sees us, and from that seeing provides what we need.* The need to feel seen is core to humanity. It begins with our wee babe selves who are wholly unable to meet their own needs. They *must* gain the attention of an adult or they will die. The need to be seen and cared for is that important, that powerful. Our very lives depend on it.

The adult version is not so dire from a physical perspective— we can lift our own heads now and manage to feed and clothe ourselves (at least on most days). But it will always be dire from the perspective of our hearts. Many of you know what it is like to go through life feeling invisible or being seen only as the answer to someone else's need or desire but not for who you are in your own right. This happens in our marriages, friendships, churches, and places of work.

There is a vast difference between being valued for our knowledge, skills, competency, and caretaking versus being valued for our existence and seen as lovely and precious apart from our doing. The truth is that you have many skills, much to offer, and a heart that spends itself in kindness and goodness. Wounded people are drawn to that truth like camels to water. The beauty and glory of your life are attractive. But having people appreciate you for your skills doesn't necessarily mean that your heart feels seen. Feeling seen requires that the other person moves toward us for our sake and not just because it benefits them. We sense that difference in the moments of our own need when others seem not to notice or move toward it.

My older adult self belatedly recognizes that many of the relational missteps I've made occurred because my starved soul mistakenly thought in that moment that I was standing with someone who maybe actually *got me* this time. Someone who noticed parts of me that had been hidden away in fear or from having experienced rejection. When it actually happens that someone sees us well, it is such a powerful experience—like having trudged through a desert with no water and no relief from the blazing sun, and then finding yourself in the shady bliss of an oasis. My soul rushes to drink there. Unfortunately, the *rushing* part can result in running past the signposts of good sense without stopping to read them. Sometimes I fail to perceive that the other person is only paying attention to the parts of me that have benefits for them. I have promised my heart to do better. I owe it that.

It is such a relief to be loved by the Trinity as there are no warning signposts that need to be read. There is only El

Shaddai and Ruach HaKodesh who truly see me through the clear eyes of a mother's love. They see it all—the shiny, jeweled brilliance of my life that is a reflection of Theirs, and the torn, ragged places where daggers have pierced and thorns have torn me. Mama God hears the quiet sobbing of my heart and the loud ugly-cry wails. She sees my dreams and passions and the road that lies ahead of them. And in Her seeing of my life, She opens Herself and invites me into Her embrace. This, dear one, is comfort, caring, and nurturing.

One of the things we have to fight hard against is the very strong feeling that what we experience here on this physical plane is Reality and Truth when in fact, our experiences are only reality and truth. The difference between the two doesn't lessen the pain of now. It doesn't keep our ears from hearing the messages in the pain, but what Truth and Reality help us hold onto is that our experiences in this very temporal and fallen place are not what define us; they are not the last word over our lives. Nor do they tell the whole or even an accurate story. Ruach HaKodesh comes into these moments of pain and opposes our enemy's whispers. She tells us there is healing for our hearts. She tells us that this season will give way to the newness of spring. She reminds us who we are and Whose we are. "Here, child, let Me tend your wounds. I'll sit with you while you cry, and then I'll dry your tears. You will be OK, child. It won't hurt forever. Those people who hurt you have no idea who you are or what they've done. Remember, you are made to look just like your Mama and your Daddy—you're glorious child, beautiful and strong. And the highways of heaven run through your life. Your King defends you, and your enemies will have to deal with Him. Rest here awhile with Me, then let's get back up and finish the race together."

Perspective is part of what comforting offers. When we're in pain or standing in disappointment, betrayal, abandonment, or loss, we tend to see through the lens of those feelings. We are tempted to hear through the filter of despair and hopelessness or accusation and judgment. What we need in those moments is a perspective that stands outside of our pain. That higher vantage point still sees our hurt, but it also sees the big picture of kingdoms clashing—an enemy who has purposed to kill, steal, and destroy your life and the victorious Trinity who comes with a sword to make peace for you. The higher perspective sees what's coming—all things made new—and not just what is. Will you let your heart lean into that? Take a moment and rest in the lap of El Shaddai, feeling Her heartbeat and allowing Her warmth to surround you. Let Ruach HaKodesh tell you what She knows and how She sees you. Be held in hope and encouraged in the certainty of all the goodness God has in store for you.

> *Ruach HaKodesh, I choose to surrender my perspective of pain to Your perspective of Truth. Heal my heart and wash it clean of the whisperings of my enemy who came as an opportunist in the midst of the hard that has beset me. Show me what You see—take me up to where You stand and let me feel the winds of hope on my face. Strengthen what has been broken and put out of joint in me so that I can run with You. Break every shackle that has pinned my feet to the earth and lift me up to Your high places.*
>
> He makes my feet like [hinds' feet
> [able to stand firmly and tread safely on paths of testing and trouble];
> He sets me [securely] upon my high places.
> (Psalm 18:33 AMP)

Chapter 7

The Great Why

---❦---

> Draw me away with you and let us run together!
> Let the king bring me into his chambers.
> —Songs of Songs 1:4 AMP

I said earlier that my desire is for you to know why you exist. Does your life have a reason, a purpose, a meaning, and would it matter whether or not you lived in that purpose? The most basic answer is that you exist so that the Trinity can pour out Their love on you, and you can love Them back in return. I want to make sure I say this first and clearly because in a bit we'll talk about all the good stuff you're meant to *do*. But before the doing, there is simply the *being*, the *loving*, and the *union*. The Trinity did not create you to use you. You're not a tool or a means to an end. As incredible as it may seem, your biggest *why* is about your heart. At some level, you probably already know this, for in the heart of every woman is the deep-seated desire to be loved and cherished and to pour out love on another. This is true of men as well, but their story is for another day.

What may surprise you is that the Trinity has the same deep-seated desire. I know, I know, we're taught that God needs nothing and most certainly does not need us. Most theology avoids the picture of the Trinity as having longings and desires but bear with me for a moment. Throughout scripture, the Trinity presents themselves in relationship with one another and also with us. Scripture gives us a complete picture of the Trinity's experience of the peaks and valleys of love. There are many passages where God responds to us as would a scorned lover betrayed by the one He loves (e.g., the book of Hosea; Ezekiel 16:15–59). Or as a father, rejected by ungrateful and prodigal children (e.g. Deuteronomy 32; Luke 15:11–32). Scripture is clear that these moments are hurtful to God, bringing pain to the heart of the Trinity. Remember God standing in a moment of grave pain early in the story of the world, saying that the Trinity regretted having made us because we had grieved and broken their hearts (Genesis 6:6). Then in a very different moment, Zephaniah 3:17 (MEV) gives this portrait of God, "The LORD your God is in your midst, a Mighty One, who will save. He will rejoice over you with gladness, He will renew you with His love, He will rejoice over you with singing." The entire book of the Song of Songs is a metaphor of God as a lover pursuing the heart of His bride and the desire that awakens in her for her Lover. Does any of this sound like a God without longings and desires?

Love never exists in a vacuum. It is always directed toward something or someone. Love must, in order to be love, pour itself out on a beloved. And you, daughter, are that beloved. The most significant thing you will ever *do* is to let yourself *be* loved by God. Be moved by that, undone by that. Allow your heart to receive without protest, the adoration of the Trinity who has set *all* of Their affection on you. Do you see, dear one, this is the answer to our wildest dreams, and it is where our own heart's desire for love began. The longings of your heart will never make sense to you 'til you understand that they are a mirror of God's heart, of deep calling to deep.

We live in a culture that has tried to shame and minimize

love. The insinuation is often that the pursuit of love over things like success, money, and ambition is immature or unhealthy in some way. It looks too vulnerable, too raw. To be consumed by love leaves us undone if we throw guardedness to the wind and love with our whole hearts. Yet this is the exact picture of the most powerful and accomplished Being who has ever been. Father God throws dignity to the wind to run down the driveway, robes flapping in the breeze, to scoop up a son who had been lost and now was home. Or this,

> For you reach into my heart. With one flash of your eyes I am undone by your love, my beloved, my equal, my bride. You leave me breathless—I am overcome by merely a glance from your worshiping eyes, for you have stolen my heart. (Song of Songs 4:9 TPT)

We have stolen the heart of God! How can this be? It is unthinkable in traditional theology, and as a result, much church culture has avoided viewing the Song of Songs as an allegory of the Trinity and humankind. But that approach would also require us to discard the book of Hosea and every other passage where God clearly speaks as a Lover to His people. Why would we do such violence to scripture? Remember that the entirety of scripture is meant to reveal the Trinity and the love story They are writing about the creation They have made from love, by love, and for love.

You, daughter, have stolen the heart of God. The Trinity is undone by your love and by your heart turned toward Them. Your worship moves the heart of God. Your choice to join your life to Theirs reaches into the heart of the Trinity. If in no other way, this is how your existence matters. In a spontaneous moment during the song "Closer," Steffany Gretzinger (Bethel Music) sings of God, "You could love me more in a moment than other lovers could in a lifetime." Do you know this yet?

Has your heart figured out that your longing for love will never be fully met in this place and time by these people but only in the heart of God?

Scripture tells of a woman who has learned this lesson and who had, in response, become an extravagant lover of Jesus. In a moment of abandon and wholeheartedness, she poured out a vial of perfume on Jesus's feet that cost her a whole year's income. Like today, her poured-out love was ridiculed by those who witnessed it; they called it a waste—all except Jesus, who had a very different response. He told those who watched that she had done a beautiful thing for him and that "wherever this gospel [of salvation] is preached in the whole world, what this woman has done will also be told in memory of her [for her act of love and devotion]" (Matthew 26:13 AMP). Can you imagine how that moment might have felt to Jesus? He had lived his whole life in the service of loving us and was about to give up His life for the sake of that same love. Jesus lived ridiculed and misunderstood by friends, family, and complete strangers. He had done and was about to do something that his closest friends only barely understood. Yet here was this woman *who saw Him and loved Him with all of her heart.* She didn't just pour out her perfume on Him. She poured out her heart just as Jesus had done for her.

Dear one, don't you want that to be you? Don't you want to be the one who sees Jesus for all that He is and all that He has done, and whose response is one of gratitude, adoration, and love? This is the gift you have to offer God—your own heart, your *whole* heart with nothing held back and no care for how it might look to anyone else. Jonathan and Melissa Helser have written a song called "Without Caution." Its bridge says,

> No more limits on my love
> Without caution I will come and pour my love on You

> I break the bottle of my praise and I give it all
> without restraint
> I *waste* my life on You. (Emphasis mine)

Daughter, what do you want to pour yourself out on? Is it worth your heart's devotion? Be careful how you choose the object of your affection because we become like the things we love. They begin to define us.

> *Jesus, I want to love You without caution or restraint, with my whole heart. And I want to fully experience Your love for me. Clear anything out of the way that has caused me to pull back from Love's gaze. Make my heart ready for love— ready to take it in and ready to pour it out.*

Living this way is transformative. It causes us to see the world through different eyes. Luke 2:22–38 tells the story of Jesus being brought to the temple by his parents at eight days of age to be presented to the Lord. The temple is full of people, and we can assume that most of them had at least one functional eye, yet only two of them saw Jesus for who He was. Anna is one of those people. Scripture describes her as a prophetess and says that after the death of her husband, she chose to give herself over to ministering to and worshiping God. In fact, she lived at the temple so that she could spend her days and nights pouring herself out on God in much the way that the woman with the perfume would do some thirty years later. Anna understood this moment and saw it as the move of God that had been foretold hundreds of years before. A lifetime of intimacy with God caused her heart to be able to see what physical eyes could not. Now encountering Jesus as an in-the-flesh reality, Anna recognized Him as the One she had loved up to that moment only through eyes of faith.

This is part of the transformative fruit of receiving the love of the Trinity and giving yourself over to it. You become God's intimate. The Trinity tells you Their plans and invites you into Their secret places (e.g., John 15:12–15, Daniel 2, Psalm 25:14). It becomes easier to recognize God in your own life as well as in the events taking place in the world. We can see these truths played out on a smaller scale in our human relationships. Living with another in loving intimacy leads to trust that allows us to share our secrets. We are invited into spaces of our beloved's heart and mind that most people can't access. And we easily recognize them from afar; we know their voices and their smell even when they are out of our sight. This same intimate familiarity can also exist in our relationship with God.

Scripture records that there were other women who were changed by their encounters with Jesus—encounters that left them healed, forgiven, seen, and valued. These women, in love and gratitude, ministered to Him throughout the three years leading up to His death. They were present at the crucifixion, stayed afterward to see Jesus's body laid in the tomb, and went back later to anoint His body with burial spices. Can you see the love in the way they lived toward Him? Like Anna in the temple, their lives were given over to ministering to the heart of Father God through their care of His Son. Such love was not even deterred by His death or their grief and confusion. Still they attended Jesus, intending to pour themselves out for Him one last time. But instead of finding his lifeless form in the tomb, they ran straight into the King of Life who honored them by revealing Himself to them and by trusting them with the news of His resurrection.

Try to imagine this moment. The women have come in the company of their sisterhood and the privacy of their collective grief. This wasn't a public display. It was at dawn when they expected to encounter no one but the guards who kept watch over the tomb. To say that they are sad is an understatement. Their lives have been rocked to the core. Things have not turned out the way they expected, and the driving purpose of their lives for the past three years seems to have come crashing to the ground. The women come with heavy hearts and unanswered questions. Mind you, they aren't the only ones who feel this way. There is a whole community of people, the eleven disciples among them, who feel orphaned and alone in this moment. But those people aren't at the tomb. Only these women whose love for Jesus lived on past his death. That's what they are coming to offer that morning—their poured-out love. It is no coincidence that Jesus meets them there and reveals Himself to them. Remember that God is enthroned on the praises of His people (Psalm 22). The women's love and gratitude for Jesus had built a throne for Him in their hearts and on the earth. Jesus honors that by pulling back a veil, giving the women access to greater revelation, and trusting them with a truth that will change the world.

Being God's intimate results in being invited into adventure and partnership. Peter gets the chance to walk on water. Moses demonstrates the power of God to the nation of Egypt and its stubborn pharaoh. Rahab shelters and protects two Israeli scouts; Esther ascends to the throne of the queen and prevents her people from slaughter. And in the ultimate version of this, Mary is asked to lend her life and her body to the redemptive plan of God.

How does the Trinity ask this of you? Have you encountered the overshadowing of the Holy Spirit? What does it look like to have Jesus formed in you, carried in your physical being (body, soul, mind, and spirit), and released through you in the earth? This, dear one, is what you were made for. Everything else pales by comparison.

Chapter 8

Your Other Big Whys

> GOD, GOD, a God of mercy and grace,
> endlessly patient—so much love, so deeply true—
> loyal in love for a thousand generations.
> —Exodus 34:6 MSG

The Mother Heart

While it is a true statement that only Love can save us, the thing is that Love must be incarnate. It doesn't exist adrift in the world as an idea or concept. It is embodied within living beings. Only as we receive love from another do we become inhabited by love. It takes up residence in us as we come into union with the Trinity. Remember that this is how it was once upon a time. In Eden, the Trinity took tangible form. Adam and Eve weren't loved and parented by a concept. They were met by the living God—Love incarnate. The Trinity's invitation to us is first that we become Their beloved, saying *yes* to God's offer to pour out love on us and bring us into a relationship that is framed by love. Love's habitation in us is progressive; the more deeply we wade into

She

love, the larger its presence is in us and we become like the Grinch whose heart grew three sizes.

Love transforms both the lover and the beloved. It is interesting how that works, and in an odd way, we see it being true even of the Trinity. Consider the passage I love so much from Isaiah 49:15–16 (TLV),

> "Can a woman forget her nursing baby or lack compassion for a child of her womb? Even if these forget, I will not forget you. Behold, I have engraved you on the palms of My hands. Your walls are continually before Me."

This is a startling statement, and in much of Christendom, it would be considered heresy. Yet it is spoken by the Trinity themselves. *Their love for you makes Them different in some way than before you existed.* Wait. Read that again. The Trinity is saying that Their very essence, Their *body* (however that word is applied to One who lives in all planes of existence) is changed by loving you. Your name is now carved into Their very being. If you've ever loved anyone, you know the truth of this. Offering our hearts to others changes our own hearts whether or not they receive our love. At a bare minimum, love causes us to turn aside and pay attention to things we didn't before. *We consider our beloved; we are aware of their joys, sorrows, needs, and delights.* This is what God is saying here. From both the joy and grief of loving you, the Trinity allows Themselves to be touched by your existence. And in the true loveliness of the Hebrew language, heart attitudes always lead to action.

It is in this moment that who we are as the beloved of God—daughters who receive God's love—causes us to be transformed into the lovers of God. That in turn spills into what we *do* as lovers of God. Loving God causes us to offer love to a world that desperately needs care and saving. Dear daughter, the breathtaking news is that we are meant to be part of saving the world by offering what God offers to us and through us. We are meant to tend hearts and hurts, to truly see people, to be safe places for them, to live protectively over them, and to point them to the love and mercy of God.

As a former therapist and now a life coach, I can tell you that many of my clients would not need me if someone had just loved them well. *We can do that!* We can do that because as women made in the image of Amma God, of El Shaddai, and of Ruach HaKodesh, we are uniquely suited to pass on the atmosphere and the gaze of love. Operating in the world as mother is written into the fabric of femininity. The parts of our anatomy that allow us to bear physical life provide a tangible mirror of our soul. It isn't just our bodies that conceive and bear life. This is also the truth of our hearts. Our mother-ness causes life to germinate and develop in our hearts and minds as well as our bodies. It is present in all of us in some form, though not necessarily the same form, and this is key. We must offer grace to one another and to ourselves that allows for the outworking of our identities as mothers to look different on each one of us. The differences among us are OK. In fact, they are better than OK. It is the plan of God.

For some women, acting from a mother heart translates very literally into bearing children and raising them in the labors of love. For other women, it is acting as teacher, pediatrician, coach, guardian ad litem, and Girl Scout leader—the roles are endless, and so is the need. We live in a world where there is rampant fatherlessness; overly stressed and under-resourced single moms; early sexualization of children; early exposure to violence in the form of bullying; and the ever-increasing incidence of mass shootings, child trafficking, and the cultural loss of a moral compass. In the realities of this world, children are in desperate need of someone who will see them and care for their well-being. They need mentors and protectors, people who will help them understand their own hearts and encourage them to dream with God over their own lives. Research tells us that when children have even one person in their corner who they know is for them, it saves them from a host of bad outcomes. The larger truth is that children need a village of people to participate in their development. Not one person, not even a parent, can contain all that a child will need. To love a child well is to change the world. Is that you? Would you be Love incarnate for them?

For some women, operating in a mother heart does not have a child focus, rather it is about the larger issues of nurture, care, warmth, and safety that we offer to all sorts of people in our lives. They find in us a safe place to bring their woes, the scraped knees of their souls. They take refuge in our love for them and watchfulness over them. You've probably noticed that kindness seems in short supply lately. Especially in these pandemic years, folks feel isolated, lonely, and misunderstood. You being just authentically yourself—operating in the freedom and security of soul that comes from being a beloved daughter—can be the face of God for those around you. Do you understand that? This is what it means to be the body of Christ—for Jesus to be embodied in our lives, our attitudes, and our conversations. When we think about the concept of destiny and what we're made for, our thoughts often go to the realm of vocational choices. There's nothing wrong with that, but don't skip over the more obvious answer. You are meant to establish the Kingdom of God on earth in the ordinary everyday of how you live and move among people. St. Francis of Assisi put it this way, "Preach the Gospel at all times. Use words if necessary."

In yet another form, moving in a mother heart can be about creating and producing a different kind of life and birthing it in the world. You see this in the works of our hands as well as in the work of our minds. We create beauty of various kinds—gardens to explore, tables beautifully set that invite us in, and art and poetry that feed the soul. We birth ideas, inventions, strategies, ministries, and businesses. The sciences, commerce, industry, education, and healthcare are all places where the beauty of the Trinity is reflected through those who steward it well. I think of women like

- Margaret E. Knight (1838–1914), who invented the machine that created the flat-bottomed paper bag;
- Grace Hopper (1906–1992), a mathematician and US Navy reserve officer who invented the first compiler (a program that allowed computers to *talk*). She also was the co-inventor of COBOL, the first universal programming language used in business and government;
- Josephine Cochrane (1839–1913), inventor of a mechanical dishwasher and one of the founders of KitchenAid;
- Mary Sherman Morgan (1921–2004), who developed the rocket fuel needed to get America's first satellite into orbit;
- Maria Beasley (1847–1904), who produced an anti-derailment device for trains, a barrel-making machine, and a life raft that dramatically improved survival rates; and
- Ruth Graves Wakefield (1903–1977), who along with her husband was the owner of the Toll House Inn. She created chocolate chips as well as the famous Toll House cookie recipe whose rights were later bought by Nestlé.

I chose this list of women purposefully because of the wide range of their contributions. Some of their efforts seem grander, more *wow* in their impact (rocket fuel!) while others have a less glamorous but far-reaching effect like the paper bag. My favorite is Ruth Wakefield whose invention, on the surface, may seem the most trivial but in actuality may have the most impact of all. How many of us (me! Me! ME!) have been comforted as children or adults by a warm Tollhouse cookie? How many

She

friendships have started this way? How many batches were offered in hospitality and kindness? It is such a small thing, but one that creates a connection, bestows a sense of being seen, considers, and invites the recipient into more.

In all of these places and endeavors, we welcome Lady Wisdom to inform our work. We rejoice in the beautiful creativity of invention and strategy that flows from heaven through us. These things, too, reflect our design as mothers. And it is in all of these ways and in all of these things that we reflect the divine. We are living portraits of a God whose essence contains and is expressed through the feminine.

Anne Lamott beautifully describes this as "the shawl of moms that the holy one knit together for us along the way." As she goes on to describe it, these women are

> your best friends' mothers who seemed to think you were gorgeous and wonderful ... and the eccentric old lady Mrs. Terwilliger who took every elementary school class every year on nature walks to the salt marshes and trees hiding egret nests, or the wild math professor in college ... That mother. That mother knew things. That mother made you take UNICEF boxes with you when you trick or treated every single year, because helping children eat and be cared for was one thing good people could always do, no matter what ... That mother prayed with her children and for her children and for all scared sad children, which is, let's face it, most of the world these days. And now that mother always helps me remember other times of the deepest darkness, when we came through, divorces, cancer, lost children and health and security, and how God ... found a way out of No Way ... And that mother helps us stay calm(er) while waiting.

> That mother reminds us, "Left foot, right foot, left foot, breathe."[11]

As women, part of loving and honoring God involves embracing these aspects of ourselves and valuing them in others. Mentoring is part of nurturing. Wouldn't it have been lovely to have had someone in your life to help you discover your heart and participate in its development? Some of you had that. I surely hope you did. I hope you have biological or adoptive mothers who did more than just bring you into the world but who also guided you through it and taught you what they knew of being a woman and of offering your gifts. You may have had women like Anne Lamott described, who Ruach HaKodesh placed along your path at just the right moments. The most precious of the gifts we receive is that someone sees us and turns aside to meet us. Who was that in your life? A teacher, coach, Sunday school leader, or next-door neighbor? Maybe it was a boss, a professor, the group of moms who, like you, had a child in Ms. Everett's third-grade class, or the women in your rock-climbing club whose own abilities push yours to greater heights.

I want to pause here and acknowledge a couple of hard things. Since the 1960s in the US, we've seen the sisterhood of women fracture under the stress of changing culture and competition. It began as women increasingly ventured out into work beyond the home, immediately setting up a line of tension between those who did and those who didn't. Accusations began to form on both sides of that line. Women who chose to remain at home were sometimes seen as lacking ambition or even worse had the word *just* applied right before the words *a mother* or *a homemaker*. The corresponding accusation was that women who ventured out into the workforce and careers

---

[11] Facebook entry from Feb. 27, 2022, https://www.facebook.com/AnneLamott

were abandoning their families and therefore selfish. Both sides of the accusations are sheer ugliness straight from the pit of hell, and while some of it came from men, it also came from within the sisterhood of women. In our insecurities and striving, we began to turn on one another.

In a misguided attempt to make peace, our culture proposed that women could be like men and have it all, all at once, and do it *all* beautifully. The problem is that that isn't true for women, and it was never true of men to begin with. Men had women at home to raise their children and care for the rest of life so they didn't have to do it all, all at once except for those dear dads who found themselves as single parents. We can certainly try for the impossible, but we (both women and men who attempt it) run into the difficult reality that we have limits. The Bible talks about not being able to love two masters equally, and while the scriptural reference is to God versus *mammon*, it might as well be said of this tension between work life and personal/family life. Certainly, we can engage in both—millions of people do it every day. But there will be inevitable moments that force us to choose between work and family, not being able to be in two spaces at once, or simply running out of energy to keep the plates spinning. If a plate falls on its own or we must choose to let one go because it isn't sustainable any longer, guilt and shame are quick to enter. Sometimes they come from within the confines of our own souls and sometimes from the judgments of others.

The dynamic I've described is played out over many issues in women's lives like whether to marry or not, have children or not, and homeschool or not. These choices shouldn't have to be matters of wounding, but they often are, producing fractures upon fractures within the world of women. Those fractures tend to expose our insecurities about the *right* way to live as though there's a manual somewhere that functions as the Bible of womanhood. As though we are made with a cookie cutter. Insecurities are often covered over by self-protective dogmatism, which manifests in judgmental attitudes. In the end, the fractures among us flush up very essential questions like "What does it mean to be a woman?"

The lines of tension I've described have to do with decisions we make about how to spend ourselves and express our feminine hearts. Sometimes though, the problem doesn't come from choices we make but rather from choices taken from us. What if our bodies fail us and physical motherhood isn't possible? What if romantic love never presents itself? What if the needs of our loved ones require such extreme tending that there is no time left for a career? I think of Joanna, who desperately wanted to be married but instead lived out her life as a single woman who tended to the disappointment of her own heart while simultaneously offering gladness and blessing to friends who'd found love. Or Candace and Sandra, both of whom have had children with profound physical issues that required constant care and supervision, leaving little to no room for careers (and barely room to breathe). There tends to be less external accusation in these situations but still lots of external curiosity which can produce a sense of feeling like you need to explain yourself.

I have always dreaded the moment in meeting new people when the question is posed, "Do you have children?" It's a normal question to ask, part of discovering who a new acquaintance is. In the world of men, the equivalent question more often is "What kind of work are you in?" Although the children question comes up eventually, it isn't as much in the forefront for men as it is for women.

The question is a painful one for me, even now. My internal dialogue, thought in the blink of an eye, is *How much of my heart do I want to reveal? How deep of a discussion do I want to invite?* Usually, my answer is on the lighter side, "Nope, no kids, just cats and Great Danes." If I'm lucky, the Great Dane part will be distracting enough to turn the conversation. The more complete answer to the question is that I have no children here on the earth but have two in heaven from pregnancies that ended in miscarriages. Children whose faces I have never seen and whose hearts I never had a chance to know. At the age of sixty-two, it is still sometimes hard to get that sentence out without choking up. It is a pain that never goes away.

If I choose to give a more complete answer, it often makes people uncomfortable. They don't expect a painful answer and don't know how to respond. So hoping to be encouraging, they'll often say things like "Well, you know, there are lots of ways to be a mother." Earlier in my life, my internal responses to that were not very kind. I won't repeat them here, but I am sure you can imagine the angry, sarcastic thoughts that masked the hurt I felt. *Make lemonade out of those lemons*. Their answer seemed to minimize my pain and loss.

My response these days is much different. I have come to learn the truth of the mother heart of women and the mother heart in me; it really does take many forms, and one is not lesser than another. I had to work to believe that last bit. Over time and with opportunity and experience, I've moved into other kinds of mothering which have been rich and healing for my heart. It turns out that I truly delight in caring for animals and in creating gardens whose beauty ushers in the presence of God who walks with me in them. There is joy for me in cooking for people and setting a table that invites them into rest and community. I have a very active mind that is prone to asking why and why not. I delight in knowing how things work and figuring out ways that extend what already exists. These are also deeply fulfilling for my soul and part of how I move through the world, offering my heart and my hands.

Life has also revealed how many people there are, both men and women, who for a variety of reasons were emotionally orphaned as children. They may or may not have had physical mothers in their lives, but either way, their hearts went untended and unseen. As children, they lived scared and abandoned, with no one to soothe them and no one to teach them how to soothe themselves. Their wee selves are still there, housed in adult bodies, still scared and alone and untended. I can help heal those wounds. I can act as a surrogate mother for them, offering comfort, being a safe space, mirroring their worth back to them, and mentoring their young parts into healthy adulthood. While some of these opportunities are only for a season, some endure for a lifetime.

I am convinced that women are the best nurturers, lovers, and caregivers on earth. We have so much to offer one another and the world. You may want to consider what this looks like for you. How can you offer nurture and care to the people that God has placed you among? He has set you here very specifically in this timeline, in this season, and for these people—because your story poured out for them is powerful and healing. The Trinity in you, through you, is powerful for them.

> *What is the "milk" that you offer through your mother heart?*
>
> *How do you nourish, protect, and help others feel safe and held by your heart?*

It is also important to consider other ways in which you bear the likeness of El Shaddai and Ruach HaKodesh. I often hear people protest that they're not very "creative". I never accept that as truth because creativity is such a core trait of the Trinity. How could we be made in Their image without the same being true of us? Perhaps a woman's imaginative expression isn't in the realm of what we traditionally think of as creativity—works of art, literature, or music. But it may well be found in other spheres we occupy: in business, in parenting, in relationships, and in teaching. When we accept that there is an innovative, expressive, imaginative, and life-breathing process in every woman, it creates the possibility that there are many expressions of the feminine aspects of God housed within the collective feminine soul. Making peace with that truth allows us to be secure in the particular grace that's been appointed to each of our lives. There is room for each of us, there is a need for each of us just as we are. When we live from that heart, judgment, competition, and accusation shut their mouths. They are replaced with admiration, respect, and gratitude.

> *How are you a life-giver and in being that, participate with the Trinity in creating life?* Think beyond the merely physical. What kinds of things does your heart give or want to give life to— ideas, inventions, strategies, the work of your hands, the offering of your heart? What is being formed in you?

What if we could lay down the tensions that have fractured the sisterhood of women and instead of living comparatively or competitively, we embraced the idea that the world needs all kinds of mothers and mothering? What if each of us is a strand in Ann Lamott's *shawl of moms*, supplying a different color or texture to the weave that collectively represents the mother heart of God on the earth? And what if, instead of accusation and guilt, we offered one another encouragement and recognition? How lovely would it be to receive acknowledgment and validation for all the many ways we move through the world offering our hearts of comfort, compassion, nurturing, and life-giving creativity.

> *Abba Father, Amma Mother, as my true parents, the God who designed me and formed me before time began, I invite You to speak into the kind of woman You created me to be. How do You want me to represent You in the world? Holy Spirit, what do You want to form and bring to life in me and through me? El Shaddai, form Your heart in*

me and help me to offer my own without holding back. I am honored, Trinity, that You trust me with the world You made. Make my heart true and whole so that I can steward that trust well.

Chapter 9

Ezer

I used to want to save the world!
—Wonder Woman

Blessed be the Lord, my rock,
Who trains my hands for war, and my fingers for battle.
—Psalm 144:1 NASB

Another significant *why* for your existence comes from our introduction to Eve. Before she was ever a mother, Eve was an ezer kenegdo. This is actually the first view we have of the feminine heart of God in women. I love the quote from *Wonder Woman*. It is so brazenly grand, spoken not from pride but from a character who stands in the gifting and anointing of the mighty warriors of Issachar (see 1 Chronicles 12:32). Like them, Diana understood the times and knew what was needed—knew that the world needed saving. She also knew that part of her destiny was to participate in its saving. Diana knew who she was and what she was made for. Without that, she would never have moved to offer herself.

Remember that an ezer kenegdo is a rescuer and protector, someone who lends strong aid in the midst of battle. Images of

Wonder Woman come to mind as I write that. The movies show her clothed in armor and wielding a sword, shield, and lasso of truth. That isn't a costume she wears. It's a reflection of who she is and what she's called to. Our challenge is to understand what this looks like for each of us. We learn an important lesson about that from David long before he was king of Israel. When he first steps into battle against Goliath, he is offered King Saul's armor and sword, but they were made to fit Saul. David refuses the offer and instead goes into battle with the tools that fit him. We must do the same.

The Lord is a warrior and as such, is the ultimate Ezer. I love how this is revealed in Psalm 91:1–4 (TLV) where we see multiple names of God, including the feminine El Shaddai.

> He who dwells in the shelter of Elyon, will abide in the shadow of Shaddai. I will say of ADONAI, "He is my refuge and my fortress, my God, in whom I trust. For He will rescue you from the hunter's trap and from the deadly pestilence. He will cover you with His feathers, and under His wings you will find refuge. His faithfulness is body armor and shield.

As we step into those shoes, we need the Spirit of God to train us in Kingdom truths, Kingdom perspective, and Kingdom heart. A significant part of Diana's story involves her coming to understand that the world doesn't just need her skill as a warrior. That won't be enough. In the worldwide war in which Diana finds herself, people engage in war for a multitude of reasons—some out of greed and others from a desire to conquer and rule. Some fight to make a name for themselves while others are driven by fear. In her moment of clarity, Diana recognizes that only one reason holds ultimate power, leading her to say, "And now I know that only love can truly save the world." Strength and skill are not enough to heal what is broken

She

or turn the tide of battle. Diana cannot save the world apart from loving it. This is the message of the Gospel.

An ezer must be harnessed by Love and walk in the integrity of the Trinity or else we become some warped version of who we are meant to be. This is because Love employs different weapons of war than those used by the kingdom of darkness which is harnessed by pride, conquest, and the desire for revenge. *Love is found at the intersection of being and doing.* As such, it is what most defines our True identity, and it is our first tool of war. This is why our enemy works so hard to diminish love by characterizing it as weak or by changing its definition to water it down or twist it out of shape.

Love encourages us to develop constancy, not changing with the winds of opinion. It is not different, depending on our mood or the company we keep. This is possible because Love is not simply a feeling, prone to change. Love is clarity of vision, belief, and choice. Clarity of vision causes us to see others as the Trinity made them—as people of value who are image bearers of God and who are made to matter both now and in the life to come (see 1 Samuel 16:7). That same vision, partnered with Wisdom and with the Spirit of God who searches out all things, allows us to see with compassion the woundedness that people carry and the bondage and vulnerability it may create. Belief tells us to trust Love's weapons and strategies as well as Love's verdict that creation is worth fighting for. Choice calls on us to set our faces like flint and persevere through the cost we will pay. And yes, dear one, being an ezer can be a costly thing.

You will be called upon as an ezer, to offer your sword and shield in the protection of others and in defense of Truth. What does that look like? First, it requires that we be someone that others trust. We are talking now about character. Inherent in this idea of an ezer is the necessity that the person be a trustworthy ally and one who can correctly discern battle strategy. Note that these are internal traits—rooted in the mind of Christ and in relationship with the Holy Spirit, Ruach HaKodesh.

An important aspect of character is developed from our choice to pursue righteousness. This simply means that we agree with God about what is right and good, and we pursue those things. We adopt the kind of humility that knows that God is God, and we are not. Our hearts bow to what God says, regardless of whether we fully understand it, even if it doesn't feel good in the moment. But I'm not talking here about mere behavior modification or the religiosity of the Pharisees. This is far deeper than that.

You've probably heard it said that the more you know God, the more you love Him. True enough but there's more. The more you know the Trinity, the more you see Their beauty and goodness. There is a total lack of corruption in God, no ugliness of spirit and no unpredictable changes that cause us to not know where we stand. God does not abandon us, does not lie, and does not act to our harm. None of the things that have so terribly wounded your heart or brought chaos and terror to the world—none of those things are found in God. The goodness and holiness of the Trinity are breathtakingly beautiful. It is where peace lives. And it makes me want to be just like God. I want to be that kind of good and that kind of beautiful. Not only do I want peace for my own life, but I also want to be a place of peace for others, so my prayer is for the transformation of my heart that leads to a change in how I act and how I treat people. Ultimately, these are the things that will make us trusted allies.

> *Ruach HaKodesh, create a clean spirit in me. Form me until I look like Love. Let my words be seasoned with grace. Lead my feet to run in the paths of righteousness. May my heart be true and always teachable before You. Create in me a heart that allows those in need to feel safe and Your enemies to tremble.*

She

As an ezer, you must also learn the skills of war: praise, intercession, discernment of spirits, how to wield spiritual authority, skill to see through the disguises of the enemy, and the use of scripture as the plumb line for Truth. That may sound daunting. It may feel like a lot. But here's the thing, dear one, whether or not you embrace your role as an ezer, war will find you and those dear to you. Your enemy is not going away until the end of the age when the Trinity shuts up Satan forever; in the meantime, you and those you love are in his crosshairs. Isn't it better to be prepared? I'm so grateful for the verse, "Blessed be the Lord, my rock, Who trains my hands for war, and my fingers for battle" (Psalm 144:1 NASB).

> Let it be so, Lord. Let it be so. I give You my hands and my heart. Teach me the skills of battle. Allow my mind and heart to discern the strategy of heaven.

The toe-to-toe confrontations Jesus had with demonic spirits that produced life-threatening storms, threw a boy into a fire, and stole another man's mind are part of the *greater things* He said we would do. The stories Paul tells in Acts aren't fairy tales or things meant just for his time. The world is under assault by an enemy determined to *kill, steal, and destroy*. Daughter, your sword is sorely needed as is your good and brave heart.

My training in warfare has been a bit of a wild ride. It has brought me face-to-face with the demonic realm and the tragic effects of sin. There's been a lot of on-the-job training in circumstances I didn't see coming, but God did. In those kinds of moments, we count on Ruach HaKodesh to fill us with all that is needed, to remind us of all that Jesus said, and to stand beside us and in us. It isn't about memorizing magic words or knowing everything. It's about knowing God and stilling your heart and mind so you can listen to the Holy Spirit. You will not be in this alone, never alone, dear one. The Spirit of God lives in you. You have the very mind of Christ, and your praise invites the presence of God, making a throne for the Trinity to occupy. When the kingdom of darkness challenges an ezer of light, it also encounters the very presence of the Living God who strikes fear in their hearts.

> *Holy Trinity, let me walk in intimacy with You and let that produce courage to take on whatever battle You call me to and wisdom to let go of battles that are not mine. Ruach HaKodesh, cause me to remember whose authority I wield and who backs me as I come to the aid of those who are under siege and held in bondage.*

Don't underestimate God's backing of you. My friend Hilary learned this in a season of wicked warfare during which the enemy came at her with constant accusations against her heart. The plan was to torment her with a record of all her wrongs. God's plan was very different. The Holy Spirit taught Hilary that when her enemy came with accusations, she wasn't to engage it in conversation or defend herself, but she was to tell the evil spirit to take it up with the courts of heaven where Jesus presides. The warfare didn't last very long after that. The accuser of the brethren never wins when Love has already paid our debt.

There are practical bits to our training in warfare—strategies like learning to take thoughts captive, for much of the battle takes place in the mind. Or things like rooting out agreements we've made that were based on lies about us or about God and breaking our contracts with those agreements. And of course, there is a need to be properly dressed for battle with the armor of God.

I realize that your spiritual upbringing may have neglected the subject of warfare. Perhaps the concepts I'm presenting are new to you, or if not new, maybe you need some coaching or

She

mentoring for how to walk in them. That's OK. We all face the same learning curve. Find someone you trust who can lead you forward in these things. It is important though that you don't fall for the lie that you must first master *all* of the skills or know *all* the things in order to move in the world as an ezer. Remember that being God's intimate and walking in love are the primary things.

In truth, having practical skills and wielding a sword won't get you very far unless you are settled in knowing who you are. I'm speaking here about Kingdom truths. Here on earth, you have many things that help define you. Roles like daughter, sister, wife, mother, and friend, jobs you do and the titles and positions you hold. The list goes on and on. But your life didn't begin here on the earth. It began in heavenly planes, in the mind of the Trinity, and in the Kingdom of God. There you are known by a name that will be revealed at the end of the age. It is a name bestowed by the Trinity on those who love God and who have overcome. In the Kingdom of God, you are a daughter of the King, a princess of the realm. And soon, you will be part of the bride of Christ, queen, and partner forever to the King of Kings, reigning with Him over all of creation. The Trinity considers you a much-trusted friend. You are clothed with the same righteousness that Jesus wears. Yours is not a junior version of that. *The Trinity has clothed you with Themselves.* All authority and power have been given to Jesus, and He has put it in your hands to use. You've been given the keys of the kingdom and the authority to use them—authority over evil spirits, authority to heal diseases and sickness and to raise the dead, authority to bind, and authority to loose. These are some of the works of an ezer.

Authority is rooted in identity. This is why you must know who you are. I love the scene from *The Lord of the Rings* in which Gandalf opposes a demon on a narrow bridge spanning a deep gorge. The demon seeks to kill those Gandalf protects, and the only way to reach them involves getting past Gandalf. As Gandalf turns to face the demon, he issues this declaration,

> "You cannot pass. I am a servant of the Secret Fire, wielder of the flame of Anor. The dark fire will not avail you, flame of Udûn. Go back to the Shadow! You shall not pass!"[12]

Do you see? Gandalf knows who he is and whose he is. His identity conveys authority, and that authority fills his weapons of warfare. It is no different for you and me. The Passion Translation renders parts of Proverbs 31 using these phrases, "a woman of strength and mighty valor ... She wraps herself in strength, might, and power in all her works ... Bold power and glorious majesty are wrapped around her." Your enemy knows who you are. What darkness is counting on is that you don't.

I realize how jarring some of this might sound. There you were minding your own business, doing life with whatever that contains—marriage, children, job, friends, pickleball, laundry, and carpool. And now I'm talking about you wielding a sword and going into battle for those you love—kingdoms, angelic forces, the clashing of darkness and light. It can feel surreal set up against the smaller story of our seemingly ordinary lives. Daughter, you cannot afford to underestimate your situation or your own life. The Trinity has entrusted creation to you and placed you here at this point in the timeline of the world, for such a time as this. You must live with the eyes of your heart wide open.

Just as there are many good and right expressions of femininity, there are also many expressions of life as an ezer. Carolyn Custis James writes, "My three little nieces are just starting out in life, but they are *ezers* too. I regularly hear from moms engaged in fierce battles for their kids. A young single

---

[12] Lord of the Rings: Fellowship of the Ring, George Allen & Unwin (1954) by J.R.R. Tolkien

She

is battling for the souls of women in Ghana, as another woman launches a new consulting business on the home front. A friend of mine faces huge challenges in his business and is stronger and wiser in his own battles because of his *ezer*-warrior wife. An *ezer* in her nineties ministers actively to lost souls in her extended care facility." [13] What does this look like for you? What are the opportunities in your path to offer yourself in advocacy for others? Perhaps this verse from Proverbs will give you a place to begin.

> She stretches out her hands to help the needy
> and she lays hold of the wheels of government.
> She is known by her extravagant generosity to
> the poor, for she always reaches out her hands
> to those in need. (Proverbs 31:19–20 TPT)

I would add here that there are different kinds of *poor* and *in need*. Certainly, the literal version of that—financial poverty and need but also poverty of spirit, need of relationship, spiritual impoverishment (those who have not yet met the kindness, love, and mercy of God), those in need of being seen and valued. The picture here is of a woman who is active in the natural scope of her life. The generosity and helpfulness she extends are not just things she does; *they are born of who she is.* This is what has been written on her heart.

One of the ezer forms that has been on public display lately is that of truth-teller and pursuer of justice. As usually happens, larger culture offers a counterfeit version of truth-telling and the pursuit of justice. What makes it a counterfeit is that it isn't harnessed by Love or in line with the principles and Truths of the Kingdom of God. But there is a Kingdom version of this anchored in verses like

---

[13] The Return of the Ezer, Missio Alliance (2005) by Carolyn Custis James

> Learn to do good; Seek justice, Rebuke the oppressor, Obtain justice for the orphan, Plead for the widow's case. (Isaiah 1:17 NASB)
>
> He has told you, mortal one, what is good;
> And what does the LORD require of you but to do justice, to love kindness,
> And to walk humbly with your God? (Micah 6:9 NASB)

In 1942, Bayard Rustin coined a term, which would later become the title of a Quaker pamphlet, *Speak Truth to Power*. The pamphlet was aimed at nonviolent advocacy. We're talking here about the kind of championing that happens on both small and large stages. In our everyday lives, there are myriad ways to live integrous and just lives that are rooted in love and defined by what the Trinity has determined as Truth. We encounter those opportunities on the playground, standing up for the child who is being bullied and tormented. In elder care facilities, we are watchful of our loved ones and advocate for their competent and compassionate care. Whether at work, at school, in our communities, or in our churches, we call out policies and decision-making, which are biased toward markers like skin color, ethnicity, gender, or age—protecting those who lack a voice, are forgotten, are underrepresented, or are disadvantaged by things like socioeconomic status or lack of education. These don't have to be loud, public battles (though they certainly can be if that's what you are called to). I'm talking here about everyday occurrences where we can step in with compassion and care, where we can use our voices to stand up for those who lack any voice, and where we can spend ourselves in kindness, ministry, intercession, and ferocious love.

Living this way does sometimes put you in the thick of things. And you'll likely encounter resistance. It probably won't surprise you to hear that I've been called *disruptive* on occasion. I can make people feel uncomfortable by asking questions like "What's that about?" and "Is that really true?" As someone who used to care deeply about what others thought of me, it was a difficult thing for me to choose to offer myself as the voice of disruption. As someone who now cares less about what others think of me, it is something I can own without self-disparaging. I am a truth-teller, and that is often disruptive. It is part of how God made me, and for me to shy back from that lacks courage and creeps into people-pleasing. The key is to speak the truth *in love*. For that, I need the wisdom of Ruach HaKodesh and the maturity not to run headlong into battle before asking God if I should and what it should look like.

> *Holy Trinity, I want to be, to live, as You've made me to be—full of courage and compassion, fearless in battle, and a champion of those who need care and representation. I want to be a woman of strength and mighty valor who is bold in Your power and clothed in Your glorious majesty. What does that look like in my life? What are the battles You call me to? I sanctify and set apart my voice to You. Teach my words to be tempered by Love.*

Ezer-ing in Marriage

> Her husband has entrusted his heart to her. All throughout her life she brings him what is good and not evil. (Proverbs 31:11–12 TPT)

We have an amazing opportunity to bring down the stronghold that was created by Eve's sin against Adam. What might it look like to love your Adam well as the ezer you were meant to be for him? The potential fruit of that is profound.

It could include healing and making repair of the core heart wound Adam sustained from Eve's betrayal of him. It could also mean the healing of Eve's heart wound from having acted as a betrayer. Much of the dysfunctional and destructive dynamic between men and women could be arrested if this stronghold was brought down. And you, daughter, have a role to play in that.

I probably need to say here at the beginning that being an ezer to your husband is not quite the same as being his wife. Let me give you a moment to absorb that. *Selah.* Deep breath. Here we go. Being an ezer is lived out in a variety of contexts, one of which is marriage. But even in marriage, being an ezer and being a wife are different things. That is to say that there are aspects of being a wife, like sexual intimacy, which have nothing to do with being an ezer.

The role of a wife is one that varies widely from marriage to marriage as it is, in many ways, the product of things specific to each husband and wife. In some families, wives assume responsibility and effort for the running of the household: cooking, chores, errands, and bill paying—while in other families, those responsibilities are divided in some other way between the spouses. Some families task wives with the primary care of child rearing while others take a more egalitarian approach to that. One of my friends is a stay-at-home dad, and his wife is the primary income maker. Wives often serve as the social connector for the husband and family though this too may vary from marriage to marriage, partly as a function of the individual personality styles of the spouses and partly reflective of opportunities for social connection. These things are the negotiables of marriage. Being an ezer is not.

Carolyn Custis James speaks to some of the differences between ezer and wife in her book *Half the Church*, "God didn't create the woman to bring half of herself to His global commission or to minimize herself when the man is around. The fanfare over her is overblown if God was only planning for her to do for the man [those] things he was perfectly capable of doing for himself or didn't even need. The man won't starve without her. In the garden, he really doesn't need someone to do laundry, pick up after him, or manage his home. If Adam must think, decide, protect, and provide for the woman, she actually becomes a burden on him—not much help when you think about it. The kind of help the man needs demands full deployment of her strength, her gifts, and the best she has to offer. His life will change for the better because of what she contributes to his life. Together they will daily prove in countless and surprising ways that two are always better than one."

Much of what James writes in that passage flies in the face of the culture of the church and even our larger ethnic, geographical, political, and global cultures. But is it true? Does this line up with the culture of Eden which was meant to be Earth's reflection of the Trinity and Their Kingdom? Well, if we're talking about Eve's role as an ezer, the answer must be yes. Remember our conversation earlier about the ezer kenegdo—a trusted ally in battle, someone as Brad Gray says, who "questions, confronts, challenges, and holds another accountable." Eve is Adam's co-laborer in God's initiative to bring heaven to earth. She is, like Adam, charged with the administration of the earth and with ruling and reigning in God's name as love-harnessed kings and queens. This is a true partnership in which each party has a role in providing, protecting, and deciding. There is no suggestion in the story of Eden of a power hierarchy. Remember, Adam and Eve, joined together and with God are meant to reflect the operation of the Trinity where none is more or less than the others.

This may be a new way for you to think about marriage or about yourself in marriage. Admittedly, it's a challenge to strip off what's been handed us by generations of culture and peel things back to the question, "How was it meant to be once upon a time?" This is an important question because the earth we've become so accustomed to is very different from what the Trinity intended. Our familiarity with and acceptance of the dynamics of a fallen world often keeps us from challenging what it offers as truth.

So let me turn your head upside down one more time. I mentioned earlier that there was no power or authority differential between Adam and Eve during their time in Eden. The way this played out is that it is only *after* the fall of Eden, *after* they choose sin that a hierarchy is instituted. It was part of God's consequence for Eve in her sin against Adam. She misused her influence as a wife, and *for that reason*, God gave Adam a position over her in their husband-wife dynamic (not in her role and design as an ezer). But hear that this was not the original plan of the Trinity any more than was eating meat or people's lives being cut short by death. At the end of time, when all things are renewed, these temporary things will fall away, and Eden's original culture will be fully restored. Ultimately, only Jesus will have headship while the rest of us will live in mutual submission to the Trinity and to one another.

So what does it look like then to live as an ezer kenegdo within marriage in the here and now? There seem to be two major pieces to this. The first is the role of ezer in the context of battle. Remember that this is about allies joining together in war. One of the reasons we need ezers is that warfare may be particularly intense and too much for a person to engage on their own. Don't view that truth as indicating weakness. We are meant to need one another (remember the thing about it not being good to be alone!). This is even described as true among the angels. For example, the tenth chapter of the book of Daniel describes a conversation between Daniel and the angel Gabriel in which Gabriel says that his coming to Daniel was delayed due to spiritual warfare. Another angel Michael had to come to his aid—an example of an ezer. Sometimes our enemy strikes on multiple fronts at once, and we don't see all of the attacks. Allies can watch out for our blind spots and cover our backs. The enemy uses a very subtle and covert strategy. Remember that Satan is the father of lies and so is also a master of deceit, disguise, and illusion. In these cases, it is helpful to have an ally close at hand to help sort through what is coming at you. All of these are examples of the kind of aid you can lend your spouse.

Ideally, you have a husband who is a son in the Kingdom of God, awakened to the reality of spiritual warfare and the presence of an enemy, and is willing to engage in that. In this case, ezer-ing involves the two of you listening to the Holy Spirit—each offering what they hear and honoring what has been revealed to the other. Because this is collaboration and partnership, the process will also likely involve asking your spouse to seek confirmation from the Trinity for a direction you sense, or them asking you to do the same.

Acting as an ezer is also about joining your unique gifting together in order to have the most effective battle plan. For example, perhaps one of you has more prophetic or seer gifting and so a clearer sense of what's ahead on the path. Another might be more able to discern spirits. One of you may be gifted in encouragement and the other more in faith. It is important to have a sense of your own gifting as well as the other person's. This requires ongoing conversations about what God is doing in each of you. The Holy Spirit continues to give and to develop gifting over our lifetime, so this isn't a discussion to have only once in your lives together. We are each individually responsible for stewarding what the Holy Spirit has entrusted to us—seeking mentors for it, developing the character that can sustain it, and bravely practicing it in the real world. Spouses can play an important role in encouraging and participating in that journey.

It is important to say that differences in gifting are not a matter of value. In other words, certain giftings are not lesser in importance than others. Scripturally, the idea has always been a multifaceted body in which every part has a role to play and a place of importance and honor. That same model extends to marriage. Men and women, husbands and wives are coheirs in Christ.

We've been speaking about an ideal scenario where spouses are *equally yoked*, but what if they're not? What if you're married to someone who either isn't yet part of the Kingdom of God or who for whatever reason, is spiritually asleep or in rebellion or simple hardness of heart? While you still have an ezer role to play, it will likely not be as well received. This is especially true if your partner is antagonistic toward God or the gospel. Your spouse may not acknowledge that there is a kingdom of darkness at work against you both. Instead, their lack of discernment may lead them to view events as a matter of bad luck or from a larger, more pessimistic view of life. Your overt efforts to supply a Kingdom view of what is going on may be met with disinterest, disbelief, or hostility. And even if your spouse is interested in your perspective, they will still lack the legitimate authority required to act in Kingdom power with you.

In these scenarios, you still partner with the Holy Spirit for discernment and strategy. You still clothe yourself in armor, still march into battle, and still accept the charge of acting in your husband's best interest for his good. It's the *how* that may look a little different. There may be a greater need to have allies outside the marriage to join you in the battle—friends, family, trusted Kingdom advisors, people with an intimate knowledge of God, and a Kingdom perspective who are skilled in warfare and willing to walk alongside you. Your efforts might need to be more covert if your spouse doesn't want to hear your perspective and doesn't want you to talk about such things. You will not be able to rely on your spouse to cover you effectively when the arrows fly, and it is pointless to ask them to join you in wielding weapons they don't have the authority to use. This is why having other allies is so important.

I'm not saying that you shouldn't be open about your faith with your spouse. I'm not suggesting that you should hide the discernment that the Holy Spirit gives you *if* the Holy Spirit directs you to share it. The reality though is that you may be in a *house divided*. If that is the case, you may well be fighting battles on two fronts: within your marriage and coming against your marriage from external forces. This squeeze can be really difficult. In my own marriage, my ex-husband who had at one time been a pastor, wanted to be the priest of the house (he actually said that) but wasn't walking with God any longer and wouldn't engage in battle on our behalf. He also actively put us at risk by partnering with works of darkness. Yep, I know that doesn't make sense. He wanted the position of priest without having the kind of relationship with God that would have given him the authority to actually occupy that position.

That left us in a no-man's-land position which was untenable. Everything in creation is under the authority of something—under the banner of either the Kingdom of God or the kingdom of darkness. There is no neutral space. My husband could not/would not raise the banner of the Kingdom of God over our lives, and I wasn't going to leave us unprotected and simply allow the kingdom of darkness to sweep in and claim territory. This meant me exercising my position as ezer to invoke the Kingdom of God over our lives and all that had been given into our care. I interceded and fought for us, which sometimes meant opposing my husband when his choices would lead to our harm. This often angered him, and it brought unkind words and accusations my way—an example of fighting battles on two fronts.

This leads us to the other primary function of an ezer kenegdo. If the latter part of that phrase includes the connotation of *questions, confronts, challenges, and holds another accountable* as we've discussed earlier, then sometimes operating in this role will bring you into conflict, disagreement, or outright opposition with your spouse. The visual image here is of someone walking toward the edge of a cliff, blind to the danger, and you step in front of them in an attempt to keep them from harm. Now if you've been taught a view of submission in marriage as meaning "do what your husband says without complaining, disagreeing, or opposing," then it will be hard for you to fulfill your design as an ezer kenegdo. Ultimately, our husbands' choices are theirs to make. If they are determined to walk off a cliff, you'll not be able to stop that. But you don't have to go over the cliff with him, and until that last step, you have the capacity and the mandate to *oppose in love.*

For those of you who are laboring under poor teaching about submission, perhaps this will help. In Greek (the language of much of the New Testament), there are two versions of the concept of submission. The first comes from a military application where submission is defined as *following orders.* In such a context, there is a clear authority structure that gives one person the right to command the behavior of another whether or not they like it or agree with it. The other application of submission is in a civilian context, where marriage would fall and has a much different feel to it. In this context, submission means the voluntary bending of oneself to fit another.

The garden of Gethsemane is a perfect example of that. Jesus tells Father that He wants something different than what Father is asking, *but then chooses as an act of free will, not under compulsion*, to bend Himself to Father's plan. This is a model of the Trinity—each bending to the other in honor and love. It is also the model of the Kingdom of God at large, every person submitting to one another and to the Trinity. Even more, it is the model for marriage as an echo of the Trinity where each part serves and bends to the other in love, respect, and honor. If in your marriage, your voice and perspective have been disallowed or construed as rebellion or lack of submission, you may need to consider with God that that expectation does not line up with the intention of heaven. Rather it is an illegitimate counterfeit.

I have worked with many families in which there were emotional abuse dynamics that included spiritual abuse—the use of scripture out of context or in a way that was not intended or the assertion of spiritual authority in a way that robs the other person of autonomy and usurps their own relationship with God. In spiritual abuse, there is often an attempt to weaponize scripture or to act in a role that actually belongs to the Holy Spirit. These tactics are deeply damaging to the individuals involved, and beyond that, they are part of a larger assault aimed at taking out the ezers God has commissioned on the earth.

I'm going to say another bold thing here. Somewhere along the way, ultraconservative Christianity has presented this view of husbands as *priests of the home*. This position can be construed to mean that they have greater spiritual gifting, kingdom authority, or knowledge. None of that is necessarily true. First Peter 2:5 says that the entire body of Christ is a royal priesthood—men and women alike. The only high priest that exists is Jesus. Similarly, spiritual knowledge and maturity are not a function of gender but rather of the degree to which we live in intimacy with and submission to God. We are all encouraged to seek the same spiritual gifts (e.g., prophecy and tongues). While scripture does speak of the husband's leadership role in marriage (see Ephesians 5), it is the role of a sacrificial leader who lays down his life in love for his beloved, loving her to the same degree and in the same manner as he loves his own body.

Let's return then to the question of what it looks like for an ezer to oppose and challenge *in love*. The *in love* part of that phrase is critical as it speaks to the motives of our hearts and determines the methods we employ. Truth that is harnessed by love is aimed at the other's good, so it partners with wisdom for the *whether, when, and how* questions. Just because something is true doesn't necessarily mean it should be shared or spoken. Ask Ruach HaKodesh what is wise. Patience may be part of the answer but so may be immediacy. The answer won't always be the same which is why it's important to ask the questions, "Do I share this, and if so, when?" Don't assume that a previous strategy will be right for a new situation. Also the *how-to-deliver-Truth* question matters. There is a place and time for bluntness (like right before the cliff's edge), but generally speaking, a gentle tone and word choice are more likely to be heard than a caustic approach. These help to demonstrate that love is your motive.

Applied here, this means that talking sense to another involves seeing our efforts as part of a long game. Your spouse may need time to consider your words. More discussion may be needed and more explanation on your part. How would you want someone to approach you? What would best help you to hear them? Much of that answer is bound up in the degree to which we believe the other person is motivated by love for us. If we are convinced that they love us, our hearts can lower their defenses a bit. If we are convinced that their love doesn't disappear if we get things wrong, then we're more likely to receive advice or correction. Oppositely, your intervention will likely not be well received if it comes from a place of anger or couched in attitude or words of disrespect. Neither will you get very far if your spouse believes there are ulterior motives in play.

Remember that the sons of Adam inherited Adam's wound—suspicion of Eve. If your confrontation or challenge of your spouse is motivated by manipulation or control, by anger or fear, that will come through and only serve to create or increase your husband's distrust of your counsel. We need to operate in clarity about our own hearts. Why are we confronting our partner or hesitating to confront? What is our goal in that?

Knowing our goals in the area of confrontation requires a good deal of self-awareness as we may be affected by our wounds that are not fully healed. For example, perhaps you come from a family where you experienced abandonment. In coming to fear further abandonment, perhaps you developed the coping strategy of people-pleasing, also known as walking on eggshells and not rocking the boat. I grew up in a family that was not very confrontational; it took me decades to learn good conflict skills (still a work in progress!).

Truth-telling harnessed by love must be brave because it may encounter rejection or anger. A heart that is harnessed by love finds the courage to speak and move at love's command for the well-being of the other even if that results in temporary tension. If fear of abandonment is still a significant force in our lives, it may cause us to leave our own ezer-calling in an effort to appease so that the one we love won't leave us. This is the woman who silences her own voice and the discernment of her heart out of concern that she'll be left alone if she speaks out. Operating as an ezer requires us to understand our own wounding and seek healing for it, or else our courage will be compromised.

Another wound that can interfere with our ability to oppose in love comes from having lived in situations where there was chaos and instability. Perhaps you grew up in a home where there was active addiction, conditional love, emotional or physical abuse, or mental illness. These are all situations that create chaos and a sense of never knowing what to expect. A typical response for folks living with that kind of instability is to grab for whatever control they can as a means of steadying themselves. If an ezer opposes her spouse out of her need to control rather than from a focus on the other's good, the end result will be that the people on the other end of our quest for control feel like they're living in a vice grip that stifles the life out of them.

> *Ruach HaKodesh, I invite Your gaze into my heart and trust You to know its state of being. Where are the wounds that need Your care, the wounds that steal my courage or that bring out destructive and corrosive words? Teach me the ways of an ezer. Anoint my mouth with words of Life and Truth. Train my hands for war and my*

> *fingers for battle. Develop my character to be trustworthy and harnessed by love.*

This brings us full circle to Eden. Where all of this went wrong is in the moment when Eve's faith in God fails, she loses her moral compass and spiritual good sense and then influences Adam to join her. It is important to see what was happening in that moment. There are only a few possibilities. If Eve was deluded enough by Satan to actually believe she was acting on a truth, then her invitation to Adam could have been out of some warped belief that this would be good for him too. This seems unlikely since in the next few sentences, we find them both hiding in shame from one another and from God. What we've learned from the generations since Eden is that misery loves company and that it feels better not to be alone in our choices. It seems more likely that Eve understood the consequences of her choice—she had violated the culture of God and death would be the natural result of that. She had just forfeited the Family who created her, chosen to turn her back on Them, and forged her own way as the original prodigal. It would surely be less lonely to have someone with her on her errant journey.

Of course, Adam is responsible for his own choice. He tried to claim, "The devil made me do it" (actually his version of that was to tell God it was because of "the woman You gave me," simultaneously blaming both God and Eve), but this was just Adam's avoidance of the truth. This is his own sin. It is also true though that Adam's sin was made easier because of Eve's choice and influence. Can he ever trust her again?

Yes, he can if Eve will allow her heart to be broken by her sin and then healed and made new by the redemption found in the Messiah's flow of blood. This is the importance of Proverbs 31:11–12 (TPT), "Her husband has entrusted his heart to her. All throughout her life she brings him what is good and not evil." What we're reading here is the result of a forgiven heart that can now love well and deeply, sacrificially, and faithfully. This is a heart that can be trusted and the fruit of her life is that her husband knows it.

What the Trinity set in motion between Adam and Eve way back, once upon a time, is being restored on the earth as the Kingdom of God advances. When we become clear about who we are, the One who inspired our design, and the part we play in bringing the Kingdom of God to earth, we take back the ground that was lost in the fall. Can you sense Satan shudder at that thought? It's no wonder he hates you. It's no wonder your life is opposed. This is why your marriage sometimes feels like a battleground.

There is a spiritual principle that the more ancient a stronghold is the more strength it has—the harder it is to bring down. What you are encountering in and against your marriage is the second oldest stronghold on the earth. That is a bit daunting to consider, but here is an even more important truth. The Trinity knew Eden would fall. Their plan for its restoration included Jesus, and it also included you, living under the banner of His Kingdom. Dear one, it's time you reclaimed your identity and the place that is rightfully yours. You were designed to be an ezer for your spouse and in the world.

The Trinity made you this way as a reflection of themselves. You were placed in creation as a gift—crafted with a fierce heart of courage and possessing the resources of heaven to aid those under siege and in distress. It will not be well until the sons and daughters of God are fully revealed on the earth. Creation is waiting for you, and God has affirmed you.

Chapter 10

Do-Over: Redemption and Restoration

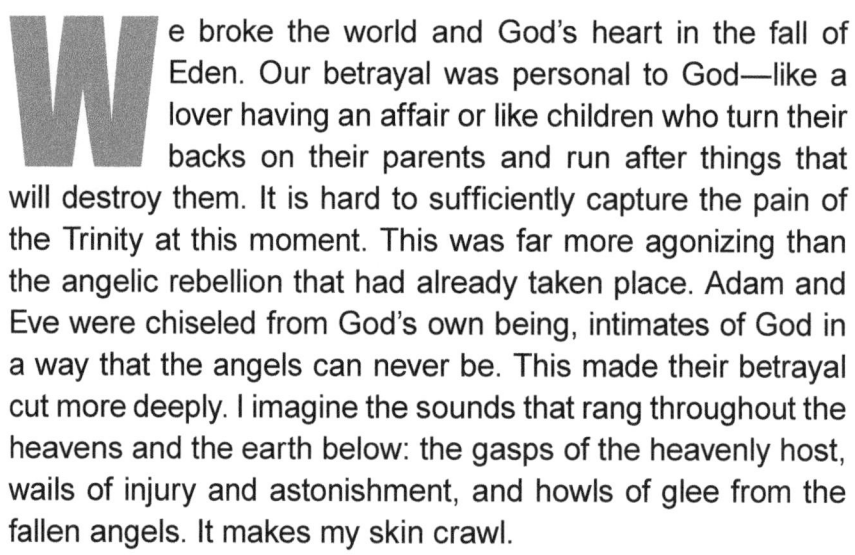

We broke the world and God's heart in the fall of Eden. Our betrayal was personal to God—like a lover having an affair or like children who turn their backs on their parents and run after things that will destroy them. It is hard to sufficiently capture the pain of the Trinity at this moment. This was far more agonizing than the angelic rebellion that had already taken place. Adam and Eve were chiseled from God's own being, intimates of God in a way that the angels can never be. This made their betrayal cut more deeply. I imagine the sounds that rang throughout the heavens and the earth below: the gasps of the heavenly host, wails of injury and astonishment, and howls of glee from the fallen angels. It makes my skin crawl.

I will never understand the depth of love in the Trinity that caused them to rise above Their pain and pursue us. It is breathtaking in its goodness, even more so because of the cost They would pay for our redemption. But then again, that is part of why God is so astonishingly beautiful—Love that will not give up on the beloved, Love that insists we are worth the sacrifice.

Bringing Down the Stronghold

I wrote earlier of our opportunity to bring down the second most ancient stronghold: the betrayal of Adam. There is, of course, a stronghold that came before that—Eve's betrayal of God. It is a terrible, unthinkable moment of insanity and poor judgment. There is nothing in Eve's history that would foretell her choice. There is nothing that explains it. She had only experienced the love of God. Remember that she was born, awakened to the gaze of Love. She, along with Adam, walked hand in hand with a visible, tangible God. They weren't just naked with one another, they were naked before God as well—wholehearted, honest, and fully given over to a relationship with God.

It is easy to blame Eve, easy to pretend that if it had been us, we would have made a different and better choice. If honest, though, our lives tell another story. We listen to the voice of fear. We are seduced by shiny baubles made of paste and things that promise to give us life but don't. We are vulnerable to the manipulation of our emotions and desires. And we have an enemy whom we have underestimated. One who is cunning and skilled in deceit—enough that a third of the angels believed his lie.

Still should Eve have known better? Yes, that is the cold, hard truth—without excuse or attempts to reason it away. And it is our truth as well. There is nothing that will justify the myriad of ways that we betray God. For us to be restored to ourselves, to the person the Trinity designed us each to be, we will need the blood of a Savior to cover our sins. Ultimately, we must return to wholeheartedness and to the position of much-loved daughters in the family the Trinity has created.

In the fall of Eden, Eve's sin pierced her own heart as well as God's. She betrayed the Trinity and also her own design and integrity of heart. The consequences of that would be in front of her eyes all the days of her life. They were present in her life with Adam, present in a life devoid of the face of God, and present in how Eve viewed herself. Once wise and faithful, she was now foolish and a betrayer. Talk about a drop in self-esteem and confidence!

We can embrace a thousand plans to think positive thoughts or believe the best of ourselves. We can engage in every kind of therapy known to humankind. We can do good works and embrace compassionate causes, but there will be *no stable recovery* of ourselves short of true repentance, the application of grace, and a return to the quarry from which we were dug, the Tree of Life that formed our fruit.

Daughters, we have an opportunity to overturn Eve's original sin by being restored to the House of God, restored to the heart of God, and restored to the Truth of the Trinity's goodness, glory, power, holiness, and faithfulness. We are the daughters of El Shaddai, of Ruach HaKodesh—made in that image and meant to walk in Their ways. I don't know if you can hear it, but I can—the howls of darkness on the brink of losing what it stole and the trembling of the gates of hell, knowing that its time is running short. When we choose as redeemed daughters to side with the goodness of God and affirm in our hearts and behavior that life is better when lived according to the pattern of heaven, we get back the authority and destiny that was deeded to us before time began.

It means laying down our grasp for control and our attempts to make our own way. It will require trusting that God loves and adores you, even when it doesn't feel like it. We will need to embrace the mystery of God, which means not always understanding what the Trinity does and does not do but believing the best and highest of Them anyway. And very practically, we must not invite the accuser of God in for coffee and conversation. This is how the serpent laid the trap for

Eve; an invitation was issued for conversation to entertain the question and the answer the serpent offered. It will come to you that way as well. Don't take the bait. You don't need to converse with your enemy, don't need to explain yourself, and most certainly will not benefit from any "perspective" your enemy offers.

Psalm 111:10 tells us that the reverence of God is the beginning of wisdom. So what does reverence look like? It begins with us acknowledging and holding true to the idea that

> everything the Lord does is right. With love he takes care of all he has made. (Psalm 145:17 ICB)

> This God—his way is perfect; the word of the LORD proves true; he is a shield for all those who take refuge in him. (Psalm 18:30 ESV)

This kind of reverence and wisdom is the first part of the feminine soul that was lost in Eden. Eve stepped away from seeing God like this. Doubt crept in and Eve found herself not trusting that God would come through for her heart. The loss of reverence for the Truth of God compromised Eve's wisdom. It led her to operate from her feelings which in turn increased her vulnerability to deception.

Please don't misunderstand me. There is nothing wrong with feelings and emotions per se. The Trinity created that part of us to be good along with all our other parts. The problem is the matter of what harnesses them. The same is true for our thoughts. This is why the Trinity introduced the concept of plumb lines which are stable Truths in and of themselves—not dependent on one's perception or agreement, not changeable by situation or the tides of the times. Truth (with a capital T) is not personally determined and speaks to an overriding, immutable, and incontestable Authority. When emotions and thoughts are harnessed by Truth, they lead us in the way of

Truth. But when they are harnessed by anything else—fear, pride, insecurity, lust, ingratitude, and shortsightedness—we wander into the brambles and deserts of deception.

We have the advantage of hindsight here and can see what Eve could not. As Eve embraces discontent, she also moves toward the thought that God is not caring well for her. Interestingly, she applies this thought toward the Trinity, who is innocent of it but fails to see that it is both the serpent and Adam who are guilty of mishandling her heart. The serpent acts purposely, with malicious intent to deceive and destroy. He uses Eve as a pawn in his game to hurt the Trinity, appearing to her as a friend trying to right an injustice. Satan's real intent is to drive a wedge between Eve and God, isolating her from love, support, and belonging and binding her to the orphan spirit. This is the moment that forms her false self. Once an orphan, she will forfeit both her authority as an agent of heaven and her inheritance in God. This is what allows Satan to grasp power over creation.

Adam's part in this moment is much more passive than the serpent's. For reasons that are known only to Adam, he chooses to abandon Eve. Although Adam is physically present and can hear and see what is going on, he does nothing and says nothing. Is it that he doesn't perceive the danger and doesn't recognize an enemy? Is Adam afraid of stepping between Eve and the serpent, worried about becoming a target himself? Or is he lazy? Somehow insecure in his ability to intervene? We will never know all of the *why,* but the result is that Adam chooses his reasons over Eve's heart. And she is lost before his very eyes.

Again we see this now in the clarity of hindsight, but in the moment that discontent enters the picture, Eve pins the problem on the wrong source. It is a quick leap from "I am missing something that is good and available for the taking" to "I am missing out on something good because God is stingy and doesn't want to share it." Enter the false self with its grasping, controlling, mistrusting, and orphan ways. This is the false self which sets itself up as the determiner of truth. "I know what is good. I know what will make me complete." The false self will take matters into its own hands by attempting to control and manipulate outcomes. And this is the false self that will quickly feel the weight of being alone in the world, afraid, and scrambling for her life and for the nearest fig leaf. From this point on, Eve hides herself, hides her heart, and experiences a true discontent and grief that comes from a shattered relationship and loss of intimacy. We have lived in some version of this ever since.

Reparation with God was not possible in that moment. There was no adequate sacrifice to offer that would cover Eve's debt to God. Her betrayal would cost her life. And though she and Adam do manage to go on together, it is not the same. There is now mistrust and resentment on both their parts. These were not just consequences for the two of them; those consequences endure to this day. Women have inherited the reputation that we are driven by emotion at the expense of reason. Men came to believe that our judgment is not to be trusted, and our motives are suspect. Marriages, more often than not, portray the struggles between passivity versus control and manipulation. Mistrust at war with intimacy. Power struggles, fig leaves, and ancient grief that we barely understand.

The same can be said of our lives with the Trinity. The Truth-knowing/Truth-telling part of us that comes from being God's beloved daughters and from our design as the earth's ezers is still at war with wrongly harnessed thoughts, feelings, and beliefs. Our trust in the Trinity's intentions tends to wax and wane depending on the outcome of our prayers and the emotion of the moment. We still grasp and control as means to still our anxiety and provide what we believe cannot be had by any other means. I amaze myself from time to time, and not in a good way, when my heart which has a long history of receiving God's goodness and faithfulness still manages to choose distrust and idolatry. I shake my head at myself (imagine that sentence in a deep Southern drawl). How? How is it possible that I entertain the notion that I know better than God? What are the vulnerabilities in me that fall prey to the lure of immediate gratification? How do I not remember that making my own way and grasping for things always ends in ruin? And how, how do I possibly lose sight of the majesty and glory of God, which deserves my wholehearted adoration and praise? I wish I could blame my foolishness on menopause, a full moon, or bad pizza, but sadly, it is simply the failure of my heart. Paul writes of this too in Romans 7:15–20 (TPT),

> I'm a mystery to myself, for I want to do what is right, but end up doing what my moral instincts condemn. And if my behavior is not in line with my desire, my conscience still confirms the excellence of the law. And now I realize that it is no longer my true self doing it, but the unwelcome intruder of sin in my humanity. For I know that nothing good lives within the flesh of my fallen humanity. The longings to do what is right are within me, but willpower is not enough to accomplish it. My lofty desires to do what is good are dashed when I do the things I want to avoid. So if my behavior contradicts my desires to do good, I must conclude that it's not my true identity doing it, but the unwelcome intruder of sin hindering me from being who I really am.

It was a revelation to me to find that trusting God in the *now* stuff of life seems much harder than trusting God for what seems like as far away a thing as eternity. God had to expose my shaky faith by asking me to walk out on a limb that nothing in this world could support—my version of walking on water or standing in a fire. See, that's the thing. Faith isn't faith until it takes a step into what can't be seen in the natural but only by the eyes of the heart.

The crucial issues are probably different for each of us. It wasn't hard for me to trust the Trinity with what I felt or thought. Truthfully, They are the only Ones I trust enough to be fully honest with. I've never come to God with my heart and been met with shaming, disbelief, belittlement, a turned head, or silent treatment. God is sometimes silent about my questions, but not about my heart. I'm never embarrassed by my tears in the presence of God. That is the one place that is absent of the pressure to have it all together.

The harder things for me have been the practical and tangible. Will there be enough money to pay the bills? What about the things I don't know how or am not able to do? Will God's companionship be enough when my marriage has failed, and I go through life on my own without a partner to share in the decision-making? I struggle with how long things seem to take and why some promises seem not to come to pass at all. Did I hear it wrong? Did I misunderstand what God meant? Was there fine print I didn't read? *Why?* Yep, I can drive myself crazy with some of that.

So here is what I've come to understand as wisdom. There are Truths about God that are factual, not a matter of my opinion or belief or feeling. Truths cannot be bent as we want. These Truths existed long before the earth, long before us. But even then, those Truths were ignored and challenged by Lucifer, the original grandiose, malignant narcissist who was deluded enough to think he was God's equal, entitled enough to believe he deserved God's honor and glory, and cruel enough to take aim at anyone in his way.

The Truths of the Trinity were written into creation. As Philippians says,

> In reality, the truth of God is known instinctively, for God has embedded this knowledge inside

> every human heart. Opposition to truth cannot be excused on the basis of ignorance, because from the creation of the world, the invisible qualities of God's nature have been made visible, such as his eternal power and transcendence. He has made his wonderful attributes easily perceived, for seeing the visible makes us understand the invisible. So then, this leaves everyone without excuse. Throughout human history the fingerprints of God were upon them. (Romans 1:19–21 TPT)

But just to be sure that we didn't miss the revelation found in creation, the Trinity sent Jesus to the earth in physical form and in view of scores of witnesses to be an in-life representation of Father. Jesus's life was meant to settle any doubt about what the Trinity thought, wanted, felt, desired, valued, or intended. Yet there were people then and still to this day who refuse to acknowledge God and who are offended by the notion that there is an Authoritative Power higher than themselves. *We* were these people until the love of God broke through our hearts.

In the everyday spaces of our lives, there is an opportunity to believe in the goodness of God when bad things happen to good people and when heartbreak makes its way to our door, in much and in little, in persecution and adoration. Even when we stood in faith and *heard from God* only to have felt disappointed. In these spaces, there is a choice to be made. The question is what it will take for our hearts to be convinced of God's love and goodness. Is the promise of eternal life enough? Not for most folks and not for me on my worst days. If we're going to shake off the delusion of darkness and walk in the true feminine soul that God intended for us, we must wage a different kind of war.

Overturning this ancient stronghold begins with being

restored to an intimate relationship with the Trinity. We need to snuggle in against the heartbeat of Abba Father and the heartbeat of Mother El Shaddai, feel Their breath on our faces, and gaze into the face of Love. Hear deep calling to deep and run as fast as we can toward that sound. Scripture says that the deep things of God call out to the deep things in us, wooing and drawing us into a relationship. We learn to tune the ears of our hearts to that sound. The only antidote to the orphan spirit is the nurture and nourishment, warmth, safety, and belonging that are found only in the mother and father heart of God. We're invited to *taste and see that the Lord is good.* This is a relational invitation, an experiential invitation. The result is that we come to see God with the eyes of our hearts.

The heart *(lev* in Hebrew) is where Truth is known. I appreciate how the folks at The Bible Project talk about this. *Lev (heart)* is "the place where you think and make sense of the world—where you feel emotions and make choices." It is the part of us that contains knowing, understanding, wisdom, discernment, feelings, desires, and affection. This scriptural view of the heart is much larger than the way we're used to talking about it.

In the English language and in Western culture, the heart is often spoken of in contrast to the mind with the former containing our emotions and desires and the latter our rational thought and will. In this view, the heart is often devalued—as though the truth it discerns is an inferior truth to what the mind perceives. We're often taught that emotions or feelings are immature and more prone to error than our *rational* capacities. In a culture that views science as a god, we exalt the mind. But let's be honest here. The mind is just as capable of error as all the rest of our being. An obvious example is prejudice, which stems from faulty belief systems and reasoning. Another is our tendency to make errant interpretations of what comes in through our senses, things like others' words or behaviors. We come to conclusions based on incomplete information or even worse, stand in the arrogance that we are able to understand the principles of the physical universe (or any other universe for that matter!) apart from the One who designed it.

Once upon a time—you know we have to go back there—once upon a time, Adam and Eve were wholehearted, *lev shalem.* They lived with a heart at peace because it was whole, unified in all its parts, and without injury *because* it was unified. Their thoughts and perceptions matched their emotions and discernment. These in turn were matched by outward behavior and choices (expressions of their will) that reflect the agreement of all of those parts. This unity was possible only because it was harnessed by Truth and Love. Adam and Eve saw and made sense of the world through the eyes of the Trinity. This is important because not only did the Trinity design and create the world, but the world itself only holds together *in Them* (Colossians 1:17). Remember also that it is *in God* that we live and move and have our being (Acts 17:28).

I spoke earlier of the importance of choosing carefully what harnesses us. Second John 1:3 is a pivotal verse for this as it speaks of the tandom harnessing of Love and Truth. What John writes here is that Truth and Love are where grace, mercy, and peace can be found. Many scriptures speak to this pairing:

> Do not let kindness and truth leave you; Bind them around your neck, Write them on the tablet of your heart. (Proverbs 3:3 NASB)

> Your lovingkindness and Your truth will continually preserve me. (Psalm 40:11 AMP)

> Rather, speaking the truth in love, we are to grow up in every way into him who is the head, into Christ. (Ephesians 4:15 ESV)

She

There is also the connection between Truth, the heart (*lev*), and intimacy with God.

> Lord, who dares to dwell with you? Who presumes the privilege of being close to you, living next to you in your shining place of glory? Who are those who daily dwell in the life of the Holy Spirit? They are passionate and wholehearted, always sincere and always speaking the truth—for their hearts are trustworthy. (Psalm 15:1–2 TPT)

> Only fear the Lord and serve Him in truth with all your heart; for consider what great things He has done for you. (1 Samuel 12:24 NASB)

In the moment right before Eve's betrayal of God, her heart (*lev*) became broken (*lev shabar*). She disconnected her understanding of the world, her desire, and her will from the Truth of God and harnessed them instead to a lie: *God has betrayed you.* Embracing that lie shattered her heart into a billion pieces. It's as though her heart endured a civil war with the parts turning against themselves. The same not-so-civil war that previously occurred in heaven when Lucifer embraced a lie now broke out in Eve's heart. And that led to a decision, an act of will that violated Truth and stepped outside of Love. We have been brokenhearted and double-minded ever since.

Redemption is aimed at healing our *lev shabar*. The blood of Jesus washes our hearts of sin; cleanses our minds, emotions, and will; and brings them back into unity with each other and with Truth. Admittedly this is a progressive work made whole in Christ and brought to maturity as we receive healing for our woundedness. It requires that all of the parts of our hearts—mind, will, emotion, desires, and affections—be submitted to a sanctifying process. In effect, we get a new operating system that reflects a different reality than that of this world. As we practice walking in this new reality, we learn to recognize Truth again. Recognizing Truth turns into loving Truth. And loving Truth becomes choosing Truth. Ultimately, choosing Truth over and over and over creates a fully integrated heart and the solidness of character that will walk away from seductive lies. Wholeheartedness—unity between our mind, emotion, and will as they are anchored in Truth and Love—is the only thing that will restore us to our true design.

I want to be clear that our restoration back to wholeheartedness is not merely a matter of discipline and teeth-gritting. This is a collaborative process between us and the Holy Spirit. Like most processes, there are setbacks, "My heart and my flesh may fail"—which are met by transforming grace—"but God is the strength of my heart and my portion forever" (Psalm 73:26 NIV). The idea here is that our hearts rest against the heart of God. If our hearts waver or melt away, they are held against the heart of One who is an immovable rock.

Being harnessed to Truth and Love restores us to what the Trinity intended in our design—to walk in wisdom. This is how we get to Proverbs 31:26 (NAS), "She opens her mouth in wisdom, And the teaching of kindness is on her tongue." Being known as people of wisdom will help Adam to trust us again. And it is what will bring people to your door in search of help and comfort.

God began the restoration of women way back in the once-upon-a-time as the Trinity described the consequences of their sin to Adam, Eve, and the serpent. In a stunning act of redemption, God bestowed honor and a vote of confidence for Eve and her daughters. Yes, Eve (and we) betrayed Them. In spite of that, God turned around and gave her the honor of opposing the one who deceived her. We are handed a do-over against the one who took aim at us. The Trinity didn't remove Eve's ezer calling from her. Instead, she and we are given a place of honor and high purpose that restores us to our original design. We are called to battle. More than that, we are entrusted with it. Can you see that?

The Trinity, who has every reason to distrust women because of our failure of faith, instead affirms us. It will be through woman that the Savior of the world comes. Not only does the Trinity trust Mary to say yes to Their plan, but They also trust her to guard the Son of God, now the son of man, with all the fierceness of a mother's heart and ezer design. The ultimate Ezer will be born of an ezer and will forever crush the head of the serpent. Redemption gets the final word. This, dear daughter, is the ultimate do-over. While Mary received the one-time honor of birthing and nurturing the world's Savior, we also receive that honor as we live lives of intimacy with God and walk in opposition to darkness.

I have waited for most of my life for men to make a way for me and for them to yield and share some of their power and privilege so that I could have a voice in the world. But I realize now that I no longer have to do that. A way has already been made for me. The seat is already set for me at the table; the Trinity saw to that. They have granted me, and all women, the same degree of resemblance to the Godhead as is found in men. We are equally made in the image of the Trinity, no more and no less. While it is true that there are differences between men and women in form and function, they don't translate into differences of worth, value, destiny, importance, or belovedness. Women hold the same Kingdom authority as men and have been given equal power and destiny on the earth.

You, dear one, hold an essential place in the story of the world. You were made by Love, and for love, to offer your mother's heart of nurture and compassion to a world of orphans. You bring your beauty and the glory of your life, your creative and life-breathing spirit. You come with a sword in your hand and fierceness in your heart to act as ezer for an embattled creation. You were born to be a Truth-knower and a Truth-teller. And you were placed here for a time like this.

> *Holy Trinity, Abba Father, Amma Mother, Jesus, I trust You in the now and in the what's to come. I trust You with what I have and what is not yet. I trust You with all that is dear and all that's been lost. I trust You, believing that You are good always, faithful always, and Loving and kind—without fail. You are righteous and true, forever. I declare with the hosts of heaven that You, Victorious Trinity, You alone are God, and there is no one like You. Only You are worthy of praise. I want to spend the rest of my life as a knower of Truth, knowing born of intimacy and in closeness with You. I seek intimacy with the Father and Mother who designed me and crafted me in the hidden place, loving me when I was a mere thought in Their hearts. Intimacy with Jesus, my Brother, Husband, Redeemer, and King. And intimacy with the Spirit of God who greets me with compassion and leads me in wisdom. I set my face to run after the Truth of You and the Truth of myself made in Your image, El Shaddai. I pledge to walk the earth as Truth-knower and Truth-teller, bringing the earth under the banner of heaven so that creation is restored to Your original plan, and the King of Kings is ushered into this place. And I receive the honor and reflected glory You placed upon my life when You made me an essential part of the story You are telling.*

Appendix

Glossary

Abba: Hebrew for father, daddy. A term Jesus uses for God as His father (also our Father God).

Amma: Hebrew for mother, mama, also applicable to Mother God.

chochma: Hebrew for wisdom, written in feminine form

ezer kenegdo: When God first tells Adam that it is not good for him to be alone, this is the Hebrew phrase God uses to explain the woman who will be created. Ezer is primarily a term used in the context of battle and applied to one who is equal or superior. It refers to a strong ally who comes into the battle to render aid. It was biblically used only twenty-two times, primarily used in reference to God and women, and secondarily used to describe some of Israel's allies.

El Shaddai: One of many names of YHWH. As with the other names, El Shaddai provides insight into the characteristics of the Trinity and the roles they play. Traditionally translated in English as *Lord, God Almighty*, its root word *shad* is Hebrew for *breasts,* suggesting that a clearer translation is God, the Breasted One. Like

Ruach HaKodesh, this is a name written in feminine form.

echad: Hebrew word meaning one, union, relationally meaning *one flesh*.

Imanu'El: another name for Jesus; Hebrew for "God with us."

kenegdo: Refers to one who is equal and similar but who stands in front (face-to-face) and in that position may challenge, confront, and offer accountability,

lev: Hebrew for heart—the place where you think and make sense of the world, where you feel emotions and make choices. *Lev shalem* is a whole heart while *lev shabar* is a broken heart.

racham: Hebrew word meaning to love deeply, have tender affection, have mercy, and be compassionate.

rechem: Hebrew word taken from racham (see above), meaning *womb*.

Ruach HaKodesh: Hebrew for the Holy Spirit, a noun written in the feminine form. This term is also used for the breath of God (the indwelling life force that the Trinity imparts).

Selah: Pause and reflect.

Yahweh Jireh: a name for God, literally *God who sees and from His seeing, will provide.*

Yahweh Rapha: a name for God, literally *God who heals.*

Yeshua: Hebrew for Jesus, literally *Yahweh saves.*

Resources for Further Mother Heart/Mother God Exploration

Below you'll find a set of interesting reads and listens, some of which I referenced in this book and others, which will take your journey further on.

1. On the subject of ezer kenegdo

    Marg Mowczko, https://margmowczko.com/kenegdo-meet-subordinate-suitable-or-similar/

    Brad Gray, *Walking the Text*, https://walkingthetext.com/celebrating-woman-a-power-equal-to-man/

2. If you're interested in exploring more about Mother God, I recommend Morgan Snyder of *Becoming Good Soil/Wild at Heart*. The following page contains links to his video teachings, podcasts, and blogs.

    https://becomegoodsoil.com/mother/

The link below is to a presentation by Morgan about God being gender-full (fully male and female) and what the femaleness of God brings to us.

    https://www.youtube.com/watch?v=orEt2pVSYZc&t=3617s&ab_channel=DiscoveryChurchColorado

3. Susan Harrison of *The Mother God Experiment* has written a very useful article on the history of the Holy Spirit as Mother among early Christians.

    https://www.mothergodexperiment.com/a-brief-history-of-the-holy-spirit-as-mother/

4. Virginia Ramey Mollenkott, *The Divine Feminine: The Biblical Imagery of God as Female,* Wipf and Stock (2014)

5. John Eldredge, *Resilient: Restoring Your Weary Soul in These Turbulent Times,* chapter 5 (The Assurance of Abundance), Thomas Nelson (2022)

6. Anne Lamott's Facebook entry from February 27, 2022

    https://www.facebook.com/AnneLamott

7. An essay for Good Friday by Sarah Bessey

    https://sarahbessey.substack.com/p/good-friday

8. *Discovering God as Mother* by Alyson Rockhold

    https://www.americamagazine.org/faith/2021/05/09/god-mother-faith-prayer-240581

9. Carolyn Custis James https://carolyncustisjames.com

Legend for Bible translations used in this book

Amplified Bible	AMP
Common English Bible	CEB
English Standard Version	ESV
International Children's Bible	ICB
The Message	MSG
Modern English Version	MEV
Names of God	NOG
New American Standard Bible	NASB
New English Translation	NET
New International Version	NIV
New Living Translation	NLT
New Revised Standard Version, Anglicized	NRSVA
The Living Bible	TLB
The Passion Translation	TPT
Tree of Life Version	TLV

Milton Keynes UK
Ingram Content Group UK Ltd.
UKHW010659030324
438732UK00009B/88/J